The Adventurer's Guide to Britain

CONWAY
LONDON · OXFORD · NEW YORK · NEW DELHI · SYDNEY

CONWAY

Bloomsbury Publishing Plc

50 Bedford Square, London, WC1B 3DP, UK

BLOOMSBURY, CONWAY and the Conway logo are trademarks of Bloomsbury Publishing Plc

First published in Great Britain 2018

A catalogue record for this book is available from the British Library

Library of Congress Cataloguing-in-Publication data has been applied for

ISBN: PB: 978-1-84486-519-2; ePdf: 978-1-84486-520-8; eBook: 978-1-84486-521-5

10 9 8 7 6 5 4 3 2 1

Designed by CE Marketing and typeset in Gotham

Printed and bound in China by Toppan Leefung Printing

MIX
Paper from responsible sources
FSC® C104723
www.fsc.org

To find out more about our authors and books visit www.bloomsbury.com and sign up for our newsletters

contents

Introduction

Welcome to

The Adventurer's Guide to Britain
– an inspiring collection of the best outdoor
adventure experiences to be found across this
diverse group of islands. Packed within the pages
that follow you'll discover tumbling waterfalls
with rocks for scrambling and pools for plunging;
soaring ridgelines through spectacular landscapes
to speed along on your bike; kayak routes and wild
swims around Britain's intriguing coastline; and
inviting, winding woodland trails where you can
find peace on the run.

We're passionate about the great outdoors
and we've worked together with local guides and
experts to bring you the best places for adventures
in every corner of the country. With clear
challenge gradings and recommendations for hire,
accommodation and other exciting things to do
nearby, we're confident there's an adventure here
for everyone. We hope you have a great time!

Skills & Equipment

The right clothing and equipment – and the skills to use them properly – are essential to making adventures in the great outdoors as safe and enjoyable as possible.

Navigation

Heading out into high, remote and weather-affected places is part of many great adventures, but if navigation goes wrong the consequences can be serious. Throughout the book we've indicated when good navigational skills are necessary, and we'd highly recommend learning the skills even if you have a GPS device. Basic maps are included for adventures where we judged this most useful, but these are no substitute for the relevant full-detail mapping.

7

Cycling

Our cycling adventures are predominantly off-road on bridleways and other permitted routes. We have also included a few road rides where they take in a particularly special challenge such as cycling around an island – or hopping between several. All our cycling adventures come with recommendations for bike hire.

Cycling is permitted on:

➡ public bridleways
➡ byways open to all traffic
➡ unclassified country roads
➡ designated cycle routes.

The National Cycle Network and Sustrans

Walking and cycling charity Sustrans is the founder of the UK's National Cycle Network, linking major towns and cities with waymarked routes, either traffic-free or on quiet roads. For more information and route inspiration, visit www.sustrans.org.uk. Route guides and maps are available from the Sustrans online shop and there's a National Cycle Network app, which is great for finding local cycleways or as a route-finding backup when you're out cycling.

Swimming

The experience of swimming in open water is a long way from that of trawling the lanes at the pool. It's exciting, exhilarating, life-affirming stuff. But with all these extras come added risks too. Here are our top tips for staying safe in open water:

Top Tips

→ Take it slowly. Splash water on your face and breathe deeply before you enter the water, then allow your body to adjust to the change in temperature gradually.
→ Don't swim alone if you can avoid it.
→ If you have health issues that might be exacerbated by cold water, seek medical advice before swimming.
→ Never jump or dive into water of unknown depth or quality. Always check for submerged hazards before entering.
→ Never swim under the influence of drugs or alcohol.
→ Never swim in water of poor or unknown quality, in particular canals, urban rivers, quarries or flooded areas.
→ Keep cuts and wounds covered.
→ Always make sure you know how you will get out before you get in.
→ Make sure you're visible to others on the water by wearing a bright-coloured swim hat and even a swim buoy - a coloured float.
→ Wear footwear to protect your feet from unseen hazards.
→ Consider wearing a wetsuit for longer and/or colder swims.
→ You can check the water quality at your local swimming spot here: environment.data.gov.uk/bwq/profiles/

Scrambling

Scrambles lie somewhere between hill walking and rock climbing and add an invigorating challenge to a day in the mountains. We have included only the easiest (Grade I) scrambles; in Britain many of these are of outstanding quality. All mountain routes are described for summer conditions only; do not attempt them in winter conditions without specialist skills and equipment. The British Mountaineering Council (www.thebmc.co.uk) has lots of information on scrambling throughout the country.

On the Water

Canoes, kayaks and stand-up paddleboards are a great way to explore Britain's rivers, lakes, lochs, estuaries and extensive coastline. If you're paddling on rivers or canals you will usually need a Navigation Licence, which you can buy online from the Canal and River Trust (canalrivertrust.org.uk) or from the local navigations office. Membership of British Canoeing includes a licence and supports the organisation's important work.

A buoyancy aid (lifejacket for small children/non-swimmers) will help keep you afloat if you capsize and a helmet will protect you from rocks. If you're in any doubt about your ability to handle the conditions you might face on a kayaking adventure, join a group or hire a guide. Always check weather and tides before you launch.

Useful Websites:
→ British Canoeing: www.britishcanoeing.org.uk
→ UK tide times: www.tidetimes.org.uk
→ Weather: www.metoffice.gov.uk
→ Where to launch: www.boatlaunch.co.uk

13

Wild Camping

Camping out in the wild is an adventure in its own right and can make many of the adventures in this book even more exciting. Waking up to a spectacular view from the summit of a mountain or to the sound of waves on a nearby shore is something every adventurer should experience. Wild camping is tolerated in many of the National Parks; however, in England and Wales it is expressly permitted only in certain areas of Dartmoor National Park and by certain landowners in the Brecon Beacons. Scotland's Outdoor Access Code gives you the right to camp on unenclosed land; however, restrictions are being brought in for some areas as a result of antisocial behaviour. Camp responsibly to preserve this precious right for the future.

14

Staying Safe

Risk is an essential ingredient in many of the finest adventures and you can't always guard against things going wrong. However, knowing how to manage problems should they arise may well prevent any serious consequences. Take a basic first-aid kit, torch, mobile phone, warm clothing, food, water, whistle and an emergency survival blanket or shelter for every person present. Always check the weather before you leave; if it's not right, postpone or change the adventure.

Ticks & Lyme Disease

Ticks are present in many of Britain's wild places, and cases of Lyme disease, caused by tick-borne bacteria, are increasing. Although they're most prevalent in the South West, in East Anglia and across Scotland, ticks can be found in most parts of Britain. Try to avoid getting bitten by wearing full leg covering if you're in a high-risk area. If you do find a tick, remove it promptly with tweezers or tick removers. If you experience a characteristic bullseye rash around the bite or flu-like symptoms, see your GP.

Thank You
~ Dune Restoration Partners ~

Warning

TICKS MAY BE FOUND IN THIS AREA

To avoid tick bites:
Wear light colored clothing and tuck trouser cuffs in socks

Apply insect repellent to clothing below the waist

Examine clothing and skin frequently for ticks

Carefully remove attached ticks immediately

Stay on designated trails
SOME TICKS CAN TRANSMIT LYME DISEASE

In an Emergency

In the event of an emergency, make sure you and the casualty are as safe as possible, and call the emergency services. Dial 999 or 112 and ask for an ambulance, giving your location as precisely as possible with a grid reference if you're somewhere remote. Mountain Rescue will be dispatched if necessary. If you require a coastguard, dial 999 or 112 and ask for the coastguard. If you don't have a phone signal, get to the nearest point of help as quickly as possible. The international distress signal is six blasts on a whistle repeated at an interval of one minute between each set. Basic life support is well worth learning about and courses are enjoyable and informative, and could save someone's life.

Adventuring Responsibly

There's a complicated relationship between those who live and work in beautiful places and the tourists who visit them. Many such places rely heavily on tourism, but along with money, tourists can also bring congestion, damage and antisocial behaviour. It's in everyone's interest to make the relationship as harmonious as possible, so respect people, creatures, possessions and the landscape. Drive and park considerately, and whenever possible use public transport – or, even better, self-propelled methods – to get there. Make it all part of the adventure! Fees for car parking and membership of organisations such as the National Trust, the John Muir Trust, British Canoeing and the British Mountaineering Council, all go towards looking after places that are full of adventures for all of us, and for future generations.

The Countryside Code

The Countryside Code outlines our responsibilities to respect, protect and enjoy the countryside. www.gov.uk/government/publications/the-countryside-code.

Symbols

Family-friendly
Suitable for families with younger children.

Wildlife
Adventures with particularly notable wildlife, as well as conservation areas, wildlife reserves and reintroduction projects – for example, for ospreys, beavers and red squirrels.

Culture/history
Adventures in places with strong cultural and/or historical connections.

Public transport
Adventures where getting to the start and finish is very straightforward by public transport, usually by train.

Navigation
Adventures in more remote and weather-affected areas that require a good level of navigational skill.

South-West England

The diverse landscapes of England's South West, from the remote moorland of Exmoor and Dartmoor to the UNESCO World Heritage Jurassic coast, provide opportunities for outdoor adventures of all kinds.

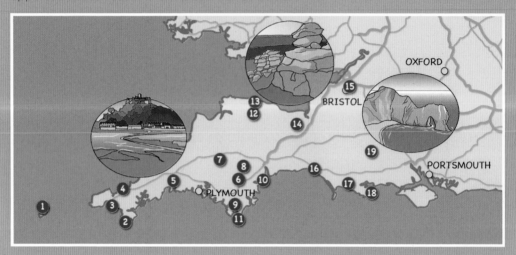

Cornwall & the Isles of Scilly

Cornwall's wild western reaches offer miles of granite sea cliffs for high-quality climbing and exciting kayaking, while there's exhilarating trail running along the South West Coast Path. Some of Britain's best surfing and swimming beaches are here too. The Isles of Scilly are just a short hop by boat or plane from Cornwall, but on arrival you may feel as though you've landed somewhere else completely. From St Mary's, the largest and most populous of the islands, you can visit Tresco, an island of contrasts; St Martin's, famous for its beaches; Bryher, wild, rugged and beautiful; and St Agnes, the most south-westerly community in Britain. The wild, granite landscape of Bodmin Moor towards the Devon border is a fine place for running and mountain biking, while to the south the intricate creeks and estuaries are perfect for boats, swimmers and wildlife watchers.

South Devon & Dartmoor

Dartmoor is dotted with tors – volcanic rock formations well suited to climbing and scrambling . There are peaceful

wooded valleys to ride and run through, numerous rivers for water-based adventuring and miles of trails, footpaths and bridleways to explore. Dartmoor is unusual in expressly allowing wild camping in certain places – perfect for a really wild, multi-day adventure. The South Hams to the south of Dartmoor is one of the warmest parts of the country, ideal for taking to the water year-round, and where you might spot seals, dolphins and even whales if you're lucky.

North Devon & Somerset

Devon's north coast is well known for its surfing beaches, and this stretch of the South West Coast Path is one of the hilliest, edging Exmoor's starkly contrasting landscapes. Somerset's Quantock and Mendip Hills are great places for walking, running and cycling, while the Cheddar Gorge and surrounding crags are home to some classic rock climbs. Exmoor is Europe's first Dark Sky Reserve, perfect for night adventures and stargazing.

Wiltshire & Dorset

The Jurassic Coast World Heritage Site stretches some 96 miles (154km) along the coast from East Devon to Dorset and is an intriguing area to explore. Visible along the eroded coastal cliffs are 185 million years of geology, covering the Triassic, Jurassic and Cretaceous periods. Neighbouring Purbeck is dotted with Iron Age, Roman and Saxon archaeological sites, while almost half of Wiltshire falls within an Area of Outstanding Natural Beauty, famed for its megaliths and series of ancient white horses carved into the chalk hillsides.

/ swimrun Scilly ⊛ ⊛ ⊛ ⊜

The Isles of Scilly are made for adventures, and in particular for the growing sport of swimrun. This is self-powered island hopping, swimming across the bays and running the winding coastal trails in between. If you're swimrunning without a guide it's best to explore just one island at a time, keeping close in to its shore as you go and well away from the currents and busy boating areas. Swimmers are near-impossible to spot from a boat, so wear a bright-coloured swim hat and consider taking a safety buoy. If you're swimming between the islands, arrange for a kayak to support you – or even better, book in with Adventure Scilly for guided trail running, swimrun and sea-swimming excursions. Travel to Scilly is by passenger ferry from Penzance, or there are flights from several mainland airports. You'll arrive at St Mary's, from where there are regular transfers to the off islands.

A great place to start is with a circumnavigation of Bryher, at a little over a mile (1.6km) long by half a mile (0.8km) wide, and one of the smaller inhabited islands.

The route: start and finish at Bar Quay and go clockwise, swimming the bays and running between them until you reach Popplestones beach. From there it's best to run inland, following trails across the island past the campsite and down to the water at the Fraggle Rock pub to avoid the tricky section around the north of the island. Once you reach the pub, you can swim over to Hangman Island, often walkable at low tide, before returning to Bar.

23

Challenge level: ✪✪✪✩✩
Start/finish: Bar Quay, Bryher, Isles of Scilly, TR23 0PR
Distance: 4 miles/6.4km
Map: OS Explorer 101

2 Run the Lizard

Running around the edge of a coastal peninsula is always a great adventure, and Britain's rugged coastline is dotted with interesting headlands that reach out into the sea, many of them more like islands than part of the mainland. The Lizard is one of these places, with a magic all its own. Even the bedrock is different from the rest of Cornwall, comprising a complex and unique array of igneous and metamorphic rocks known as Lizard Serpentinite, and supporting a fascinating range of heathland and wetland habitats. The coastline here is one of the most spectacular, with gems such as Lizard Point and Kynance Cove to discover. The South West Coast Path runs around the peninsula, providing well-maintained, waymarked running with incredible views and the opportunity to spot seals, dolphins and basking sharks. And with average temperatures the highest in mainland Britain, it's a great year-round adventure destination too.

The route: begin at the crossroads in the centre of Lizard village where the A3083 crosses Pentreath Lane and Beacon Terrace. Head east along Beacon Terrace and then Church Cove Road to reach the coast path

Local Highlights

→ Sleep at the eccentric Henry's Campsite in Lizard village.
→ Explore the Lizard by kayak – Lizard Adventure offers expert guiding around the spectacular coastline, working in partnership with the National Trust and the charity Surfers Against Sewage.
→ Refuel with a traditional Cornish pasty from Ann's Pasties in Lizard.

at Church Cove. Turn right and run along the coast path until you reach Kynance Cove. From here turn right, leaving the coast path and following signed footpaths to return to Lizard.

Challenge level: ✪✪✪✩✩
Start/finish: Lizard village
OS grid ref: SW 703126
Distance: 7 miles/11km
Public transport: buses from Redruth
Map: OS Explorer 103

3 Swim around St Michael's Mount

St Michael's Mount rises from the sea in Mount's Bay, Marazion, just east of Penzance. The swim around the castle-topped island, visible from much of this stretch of the South West Coast Path, is a real adventure, leaving the popular beach behind and exploring the peaceful further reaches of the island. It can be undertaken at all tide levels; however, if the tide is out you'll start with a walk across part of the causeway and a scramble over rocks to the water. At high tide you'll need to start and finish at the slip near the Godolphin Arms. The most straightforward circumnavigation is to swim around the Mount clockwise from the causeway, arriving back on the beach on the western side of Marazion. Be aware of boats as you go and make sure you're visible to others – a bright swim hat and swim buoy

are recommended. The distance varies from about ¾ mile (1,200m) at low tide to 1½ miles (2,500m) at high tide and there are plenty of opportunities to rest as long as you keep close to the shore. Don't attempt this swim in rough seas – the coastline is very rocky and can be extremely hazardous in high waves. For those who prefer to swim with company there's an annual organised swim here each August raising money for the Chestnut Appeal, a prostate cancer charity.

Challenge level: ✪✪✪✪✪
Start/finish: St Michael's Mount, Marazion, Cornwall, TR17 0HS
Distance: 1 mile/1.6km
Map: OS Explorer 102

Local Highlights
➡ Base yourself at Porth-en-Alls, just around the coast from Marazion at Prussia Cove, a private coastal estate. Camp, or stay in one of their historical cottages just a short walk from the beach. There's also a bakery, stonebaked pizzas, boat trips and coasteering to enjoy.
➡ West from Penzance, the South West Coast Path follows a fascinating section that's perfect for running. Discover the quiet cove at Lamorna, and the Minack Theatre – an open-air auditorium hewn from the local granite.
➡ Camp at Treen Farm Campsite and swim at the stunning local beaches.

4 Ride coast to coast across Cornwall

Coast-to-coast crossings always feel like an adventure, and a growing number of them are springing up along the length and breadth of the country. It's not often you can complete one of these crossings in an hour, but you can in Cornwall, where the waymarked and mainly traffic-free Sustrans cycle route follows the old mineral tramways north–south across the county.

The route: begin at the harbour in the pretty village of Portreath on the north coast, a popular spot with surfers (the Vortex is a well-known surf break by the harbour wall, worth checking out whether you're a seasoned surfer or simply to watch the action). From there the cycleway winds through the Cornish landscape, into the lovely Poldice Valley with its former mining areas, through woodland and the former arsenic works, and the final stretch passes under the Carnon Viaduct into the old port at Devoran. There are some excellent diversions along the way for those who enjoy their cycling a little more extreme: the Track at Portreath is a premier dirt-jumping facility, open year round; Poldice Valley Trails has a great range of mountain bike trails to suit all abilities; and Falmouth Bike Park is home to a national-standard 4X mountain bike track. There's a café and bike hire at Cambrose, near the start of the route.

Challenge level: ★★✩✩✩
Start: Portreath Harbour
OS grid ref: SW 654454
Finish: Devoran
OS grid ref: SW 798389
Distance: 12 miles/19km
Map: OS Explorer 104

Local Highlights

→ Elm Farm, between Portreath and Porthtowan, offers camping, glamping and bike hire and has its own café/bar, all within walking distance of beautiful Cornish beaches and perfectly located for exploring the Mineral Tramways (www.elmfarm.biz).

→ Explore the beautiful Roseland Peninsula, just across Carrick Roads from Devoran.

5 Paddle the Fowey Estuary

Set within the Polperro Heritage Coast, the winding river Fowey (pronounced 'Foy') widens and narrows delightfully as it approaches the sea, inviting exploration by canoe, kayak or paddleboard. The descent from Lostwithiel to Readymoney Cove takes you through a fascinating variety of sights and sounds, from jangling boats to the elegant egrets that stalk the mud flats. Daphne du Maurier wrote some of her most famous novels while she lived at Ferryside in Fowey town, the house clearly visible from the water as you paddle by. There are several creeks to explore as you go, but be aware of the receding tide so that you don't find yourself stuck.

The route: launch from the bridge at Lostwithiel at high water, landing at Fowey, with a stop at Golant at around halfway should you wish – the Fisherman's Arms pub is right on the water. The ferry slipway provides a good landing place, but be aware of the ferries crossing regularly here. To extend the trip, you can leave the estuary – take care, as the entrance can get choppy in a strong wind – and follow the coast west around St Austell Bay to land at Charlestown, Mevagissey or Gorran Haven. With an inflatable kayak you can hop out at Fowey, deflate the boat and take a taxi back to Lostwithiel, or kayak hire is available from Fowey Kayak Hire in Fowey.

Challenge level: ✪✪✪✪✪
Start: Lostwithiel Bridge, PL22 0EW
Finish: Fowey Landing, PL23 1AT
Distance: 6 miles/10km
Map: OS Explorer 107

Local Highlights

➡ Sleep at the National Trust's peaceful, eco-friendly campsite at Highertown Farm, Lansallos and explore the nearby smugglers' coves.
➡ Visit Restormel Castle in Lostwithiel, one of the best examples of a round-keep castle in Britain.
➡ Swim and scramble around the rocky outcrops at dramatic Lantic Bay – the shoreline shelves steeply here, so you can swim in deep water while still keeping close to the shore.

6 Swim the Double Dart Descent

There are many outstanding sections to explore on the river Dart, from top-quality whitewater kayaking to a 10km estuary swim. The fun double Dart descent, part scramble, part swim, takes in some of the most stunning pools, including Sharrah Pool, Bel Pool, Wellsfoot Island, Salters Pool and Spitchwick. Take care after heavy rain and be aware of kayakers, who also enjoy the descent.

   The route: start at the New Bridge car park and walk up the double Dart through the woods – some of the walk along the gorge is fairly adventurous in its own right. Depending on the length of swim you want to do, you can get in at any point that looks accessible; however, to experience the full descent continue until you reach Mel Tor and a series of beautiful, deep pools connected by slides and falls. From here it's about 3 miles (4.8km) to the Cresta Run bend at the bottom end of Spitchwick, or you can get out at New Bridge car park. If the river's fairly low you can stay in for most of the way, but you can simply scramble along the bank if you're unsure of any sections. We'd strongly advise a wetsuit and footwear for protection. Please note: there is no longer a car park at Spitchwick, as it has been closed to avoid damage to the area.

Challenge level: ✪✪✪✪✪
Start/finish: New Bridge car park, Poundsgate, Dartmoor
OS grid ref: SX 710709
Distance: 3 miles/4.8km
Map: OS Explorer OL28

Local Highlights

➻ End a day of moorland adventures by sleeping under the stars. Dartmoor National Park allows wild camping in certain areas. Please leave no trace.

➻ The nearby woodland at Hembury is a conservation area for its plants, oak trees and rare butterflies. Explore Hembury Castle, an Iron Age hillfort with a Norman motte (mound) and bailey (enclosure) castle, and spot fritillaries flitting through the trees.

➻ Stock up on picnic essentials at the Ashburton Deli.

7 Climb to the summit of Dartmoor

High Willhays and its neighbouring Yes Tor are southern England's only 'official' mountains, both rising to above 2,000 feet (610m). An ascent of High Willhays makes for an enjoyable adventure that balances dramatic scenery and a real feeling of wilderness with easy accessibility and an achievable level of challenge. This route starts with a crossing of the vast dam at Meldon Reservoir and breathtaking views out across the gleaming lake that lies nestled in open moorland, 900 feet (275m) above sea level. The steep ascent, first to the summit of High Willhays and then, via the airy ridge along the roof of Devon, to neighbouring Yes Tor, is handsomely rewarded with moorland views and a real feeling of escape. There's so much to explore nearby too, including the fascinating gnarled boughs at Black-a-Tor copse, one of the finest remaining upland ancient oak woodlands in Britain.

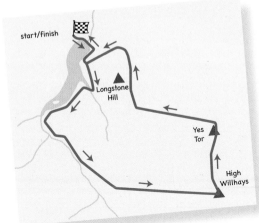

The route: from the car park, cross the dam across Meldon Reservoir and follow the southern shore to a footbridge. Cross this and follow the West Okement River for 1.5km until the rocks of Black Tor appear up to your left. Climb up to these and continue to the summit of High Willhays. Follow the ridge to the trig point on the summit of Yes Tor, from where a clear path leads down to a track along the eastern slopes of Longstone Hill. Continue

along this track to return to the start. NB: this route crosses into an MOD live firing range; full information can be found at: https://www.gov.uk/government/publications/dartmoor-firing-programme. Check firing times before you leave and never enter a range when red flags are flying.

Challenge level: ✪✪✪◌◌
Start/finish: Meldon Reservoir car park, EX20 4LU
Distance: 8 miles/12km
Map: OS Explorer OL28

Local Highlights

➠ Dartmoor is great for exploring by bike. Try some of the great mountain bike trails around Princetown or a weekend's bikepacking.
➠ Tamar Trails near Tavistock on the western edge of Dartmoor has great trail running and cycling, a café and experienced guides who can lead you on a guided run of the moor (www.tamartrails.co.uk).

Dartmoor is well known for its high-quality granite bouldering and rock climbing, dotted as it is with huge tors, the remnants of ancient underground volcanic activity. Some of the larger outcrops, such as Haytor and Hound Tor, are great for scrambling right to the top using any number of routes. For the best bouldering, Bonehill offers something at just about every grade. But when we came to look for good scrambles that combine the exposure and concentration required for harder climbing with the easier grading and accessibility of a classic scramble, there was one that stood out: Greator Rocks rise like a giant backbone from the hillside below Hound Tor. Flanked by a ruined medieval village and a swathe of bracken-clad moorland that runs down to Becka Brook in the valley below, it's a glorious place to spend an hour or two, as you carefully find your way along the long, rocky ridge from one end to the other. There are no particularly difficult sections, but the main stretch feels high, exposed and exciting considering its ease of access. There are several climbing routes that take on the steeper sides and summit at the top of the ridge, so please be aware of climbers using these as you traverse.

Challenge level: ⭐⭐⭐⭐⭐
Location: Greator Rocks, Dartmoor
OS grid ref: SX 746786
(parking at Hound Tor car park, 1 mile away)
OS grid ref: SX 739793
Map: OS Explorer OL28

Local Highlights

➡ Explore Hundatora, an abandoned medieval village last occupied during the 14th century.
➡ Walk across to Haytor Down and explore Haytor Rocks and the granite tramway, built in 1820 to transport granite to the canal at Stover.
➡ Refuel at the Home Farm mobile café in Haytor car park – great cake and coffee.

9 Paddle the Salcombe-Kingsbridge Estuary 🔵

The Salcombe-Kingsbridge estuary is unusual in that it has no large rivers flowing into it and is instead fed by a series of small streams rising high in the rolling hills of the South Hams countryside. The estuary is tidal as far as Kingsbridge, and at high tide the ria – a river valley flooded by the sea – has a number of creeks that run into the surrounding villages. There's a wealth of wildlife here and it's an Area of Outstanding Natural Beauty, a Site of Special Scientific Interest and a nature reserve where you might spot grebes, cormorants, herons and egrets. Further towards the entrance to the sea it's common to see dolphins, seals and even basking sharks venturing into the rich feeding grounds – should you encounter any of these creatures, please stay a good distance from them. At mid-high tide all of the estuary and its creeks are accessible for exploration by kayak, but don't get caught out as the tide recedes rapidly. Be aware of the many boats

that use this stretch of water. The best time to launch from Kingsbridge and experience the full length of the estuary is after mid-tide on a rising tide, when you'll have the greatest window for exploration. Land at North or South Sands, just south of Salcombe, accessible at any level of tide. Kingsbridge-based Singing Paddles works with the National Trust, providing guided excursions on the estuary.

Challenge level: ✪✪✪✩✩
Start: Squares Quay, Kingsbridge TQ7 1HN
OS grid ref: SX 735440
Finish: Salcombe, either Baston (OS grid ref: SX 739394) or North/South Sands (OS grid ref: SX 730382)
Distance: Kingsbridge–Salcombe 5 miles/8km
Map: OS Explorer OL20

Local Highlights

➡ Paddle up Southpool Creek to the pretty village of South Pool for lunch at the Millbrook Inn.
➡ Camp at Karrageen Caravan and Camping Park in Bolberry, ideally positioned for exploring the spectacular coast here, in particular Bolt Head and Soar Mill Cove.

10 Ride the Exe Estuary Trail

Cycling charity Sustrans' network of off-road cycle routes uses former railways, trails, paths and disused roads to provide safe, enjoyable routes right across the country. Cycling a Sustrans route is often a completely different experience from riding elsewhere: you might find yourself deep underground riding through old railway tunnels, exploring cuttings through towering crags and discovering places accessible yet hidden from roads and cities where wildlife thrives. The Exe Estuary Trail is a 17.5-mile (28km), fairly flat, traffic-free route between Dawlish, on the western edge of the estuary, around to Exmouth, on the eastern edge – a sweeping area of coastal marshland. This is a nationally important wildlife reserve where you can spot lapwings, redshanks and rare Cetti's warblers in spring and thousands of waterbirds, including black-tailed godwits and wigeons, in winter. Avocets congregate where the estuary narrows near to Topsham and grey seals can sometimes be seen near to the entrance to the sea. The route is clearly indicated throughout with blue signs for National Cycle Network Route 2, and there are rail links at both ends and a ferry from Exmouth back to Starcross, near to the start. We'd highly recommend extending the

Local Highlights

→ Hire a kayak from Saddles and Paddles on the quayside (bike hire also available) and explore the picturesque river.
→ Refuel at Lutzy's Café, a regular post-adventure stop for local runners, paddlers and cyclists – Lutzy's Portuguese custard tarts are legendary.

Challenge level: ★☆☆☆☆
Start: Dawlish railway station, EX7 9PJ
OS grid ref: SX 964767
Finish: Exmouth railway station, EX8 1BZ
OS grid ref: SX 999812
Distance: 17½ miles/28km (21 miles/34km with detour to Exeter Quay)
Maps: OS Explorer OL44, 114 & 115

standard 17½-mile (28km) route by detouring halfway along through the Riverside Valley Park, following NCN34 to the vibrant quayside at Exeter, adding about 3½ miles (5.6km) to the ride.

II Around Prawle Point

Set at the end of a spear-shaped peninsula on the eastern side of the Salcombe-Kingsbridge estuary, Prawle Point is Devon's most southerly landmark. This is a place of big seas, rugged coastal cliffs, rocky inlets and towering headlands, all edged by the South West Coast Path's inviting and well-waymarked trail. The whole peninsula is a joy to run, or to spend a few hours on at a leisurely walk, taking in one of the most stunning sections of the coast path. At the halfway point there's a good climb up to the village of East Prawle, where a warm welcome at the eccentric Pig's Nose Inn awaits. The pub is named after the nearby headland where an iron mine operated (unsuccessfully) during the 19th century.

The route: from the car park join the South West Coast Path and turn right, following it west to Prawle Point. Continue along the coast path to Pig's Nose Point (2km, OS grid ref: SX 76250 36219). Turn right here, leaving the coast path and heading inland following a small stream uphill to reach a lane. Bear right here and follow the lane to a T-junction with Higher Farm on your right. Turn left here and follow the lane past some ponds, taking the second right, Town Road. At the right-hand bend turn left onto a bridleway, following this to the coast path. Turn right and follow the coast path back to the car park.

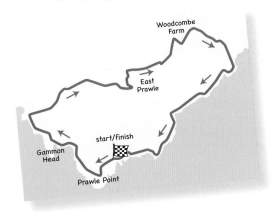

Challenge level: ●●●○○
Start/finish: Prawle Point car park
OS grid ref: SX 775354
Distance: 6¼ miles/10km
Map: OS Explorer OL20

Local Highlights

➡ Along the coast to the east of Prawle you'll find the dramatic, rocky spit of Start Point with its bright white lighthouse and the lost village of Hallsands, claimed by the sea in the early 20th century.

➡ Refuel at Britannia on the Beach at Beesands.

12 Swim the East Lyn River: ⚫⚫
Long Pool to Watersmeet

To the north of Exmoor, the East Lyn River carves its way through the landscape within a deep, wooded, steep-sided valley, joining Hoar Oak Water at Watersmeet. Clear paths run along both sides of the river here, making it a great stretch for a swim, with easy escapes for any sections you'd prefer not to tackle. The path on the right-hand side of the river as you descend is the Coleridge Way, a 51-mile (82km) waymarked long-distance walking trail that starts in the Quantock Hills and ends at the sea in Lynmouth. About 1km downstream from the start lies Long Pool, a deep ravine of about 165 feet (50m) in length. Both Long Pool and Watersmeet on Exmoor are popular swimming spots; Long Pool is secluded and leafy, whereas Watersmeet is open and easily accessible, and therefore often busier. But with a wetsuit and footwear, the descent between the two is an exciting adventure, with plenty of drops and slides along the way. Beginning at the (excellent) Rockford Inn, the swim ends at Watersmeet, where there's a National Trust tearoom for a welcome post-swim refuel. This area is carefully managed by the National Trust, and you might spot otters fishing for the local trout and salmon.

Please be aware of anglers and kayakers who may also use this stretch of the river, and don't attempt swimming in it after heavy rain.

Challenge level: ✪✪✪✪✪
Start: Rockford Inn, Exmoor, EX35 6PT
Finish: Watersmeet, Lynmouth, Exmoor
OS grid ref: SS 745486
Distance: 1¾ miles/3km
Map: OS Explorer OL9

Local Highlights

➜ Camp at Cloud Farm in the Doone Valley, right next to Badgworthy Water.
➜ Try the Rockford Inn for lunch and a local ale, or the Watersmeet Café for tea and scones.
➜ If you're a competent paddler you can kayak from Watersmeet House down to Lynmouth between 1 October and 31 March. Check the gauge under the bridge at Watersmeet House; if the water level is 'green' it's safe to paddle. Note that there is only access at set points – see leaflets available at Watersmeet.

34

13 Castle Rock & the Valley of Rocks

Exmoor's Valley of Rocks is somewhere that, once visited, never quite leaves you. It's a place of contrasts: one side of the valley is rolling moorland, the other jagged rock formations, and in the centre lies a manicured cricket pitch. On a clear day the light is beautiful – the rocks, grass, bracken and sea change colour from one minute to the next as the sun makes its way over the valley. And there's

Path from Lynton, an airy trail that runs at half-height between the rocks and the sea, Castle Rock looms ahead as you approach the entrance to the Valley of Rocks. Though naturally formed, it is unmistakably a fortress, with its lofty turrets perched above the waves. The fossil-strewn Devonian rock here is some of the oldest of its kind in Devon and enjoyable to climb on. There are several graded routes up the various faces, but the scramble to the top is a pleasant one, and when you reach it, it is a wonderful place from which to watch the sun set.

Challenge level: ★✩✩✩✩
Location: a few hundred metres from the Valley of Rocks car park, Lynton, EX35 6JH
OS grid ref: SS 708497
Map: OS Explorer OL9

an intriguing mystery here too – the Valley of Rocks is an old river valley, carved over thousands of years by the East Lyn, but now, with the Lyn meeting the sea at Lynmouth, it is high and dry without the slightest hint of a river. A herd of wild goats has lived here, on and off, for decades, and they often pose high on the rocky outcrops, silhouetted against the sky. The valley has inspired many literary greats over the years, from Wordsworth and Coleridge to RD Blackmore, who set part of *Lorna Doone* here.

As you walk along the South West Coast

Local Highlights

➜ Refuel at Charlie Friday's café in Lynmouth.
➜ Stay at the National Trust's Butter Hill Barn bunkhouse (sleeps 6, dog-friendly) set on the dramatic North Devon coast.
➜ Visit Cow Castle, an Iron Age hillfort above the river Barle – a wonderful swimming spot too: OS grid ref: SS 792372.

36

The Quantock Hills were the site of England's first Area of Outstanding Natural Beauty, designated as such in 1956. They have more bridleways per square kilometre than

anywhere else in Britain, making them perfect for exploring by bike, particularly as so many of the trails are exciting, high-quality singletrack.

The main ridgeline that runs north–south along the hills is a great introduction to the area and one of the easiest bridleways both to ride and to navigate. Smaller bridleways drop off the ridge to left and right at regular intervals, allowing you to explore further afield if you don't mind the climb back up. With a car park at either end, this is a lovely ride, taking about an hour each way. Near to the southern end of the ridge, bordered by a stunning avenue of beech trees, stands Triscombe Stone, marking the crossroads of an ancient drovers' way. From here you can walk up to Wills Neck, the highest point in the hills – the

bridleway itself continues to the north of this high point, so please don't cycle to the summit.

The route: to avoid crossing the busy A39, the best out-and-back route starts and finishes at Lydeard Hill car park at the southern tip of the hills. From here follow the main ridge track north, passing Wills Neck and Triscombe Stone and continuing along the track to descend steeply to where the A39 draws the northern boundary of the hills. Return by the same route in reverse.

Challenge level: ⭐⭐✩✩✩
Start/finish: Lydeard Hill car park, TA4 3DY
OS grid ref: ST 180339
Distance: 15 miles/24km (7½miles/12km each way)
Map: OS Explorer 140

Local Highlights

➡ Visit peaceful Kilve beach and scramble out along the long, rocky fingers that reach out to the Bristol Channel (no swimming).
➡ Enjoy a post-ride pint at the Rising Sun Inn in West Bagborough, close to the start/finish point.
➡ Camp, glamp or B&B at Huntstile Organic Farm, Goathurst – the breakfasts are legendary.

15 Bikepack the Kennet & Avon

The 87-mile (60km) Kennet and Avon Canal comprises two navigable rivers linked by a stretch of canal; starting at Bristol, it follows the natural course of the river Avon to Bath, where it splits off to become a canal that runs all the way to Newbury. Here it joins the river Kennet for the final stretch to Reading. The 100-mile (161km) cycle route follows the Sustrans National Cycle Network Route 4 and is predominantly off-road apart from a stretch along country lanes through the Vale of Pewsey and in Bath city centre. It begins along the surfaced Bristol–Bath path, a former railway route that passes a section of track still used by steam trains. There's much to see along the way, including the aqueducts at Dundas and Avoncliff and the flight of sixteen locks at Caen Hill near Pewsey, which take 5–6 hours to navigate in a boat. Look out for herons fishing from the banks and bright blue kingfishers skimming along the water. A diversion can also be taken to include the Bath Two Tunnels Greenway, another stretch of former railway that passes through Britain's longest walking/cycling tunnel. There are refreshment stops at regular intervals along the way and the primary towns all offer accommodation.

Local Highlights

→ Spend a day exploring Bristol's best mountain bike spots, including Leigh Woods and Ashton Court.

→ Take a dip in the river Avon or the river Frome where they pass through peaceful wooded valleys. At Dundas and Avoncliff the towpath crosses spectacular aqueducts, both designed by John Rennie.

→ Visit the white horse at Pewsey, one of 13 etched into the Wiltshire chalk escarpments. Cut in 1937, it replaced a much older version, now lost in the undergrowth.

Challenge level: ★★★☆☆
Start: Bristol Temple Meads railway station, BS1 6QF
Finish: Reading railway station, RG1 1LZ
Distance: 100 miles/161km
Maps: OS Explorer 154–9

16 Climb Golden Cap

Golden Cap is the highest point on the south coast of England. Its name comes from the distinctive golden greensand rock layer that forms the pointed summit of the cliff, visible from many miles away along the coast and resembling a gold-topped mini Matterhorn. In fact, although it's a joy to climb the hill, in many ways the best views of it are from afar.

You can make your ascent of Golden Cap from several directions. Straight up from the pretty seaside village of Seatown is the most direct, or park at the National Trust's Langdon Hill car park and amble through bluebell-filled woodland. The wider estate is beautiful, and there's a National Trust shop/café on site. You can even start in Lyme Regis and follow the fossil-strewn pebble beaches and ledges past Charmouth. Either join the coast path just after Charmouth or, at low tide, carry on to Westhay Water and ascend there. It's worth noting that the cliffs along this stretch of the coast are notoriously unstable – please avoid going near to their edges and bases for your safety.

Challenge level: ★☆☆☆☆
Location: Langdon Hill car park, Bridport, DT6 6JW
Map: OS Explorer 116

Local Highlights
→ Fall asleep to the sound of the waves on the pebble shore at Seatown - the campsite is part of a larger holiday park but the location is hard to beat.
→ Sample the local seafood at the Hive Beach Café, Burton Bradstock.
→ Explore the Cobb at Lyme Regis, the place that inspired John Fowles to write *The French Lieutenant's Woman*.

17 Swim through Durdle Door ⛲ 🏛

In many ways, Durdle Door sums up England's extraordinary Jurassic Coast: a place shaped by its geology into something intriguing, alluring, and yet also temporary. This is a constantly changing environment, eroded day and night by the relentless sea. The Door itself is formed from a section of harder limestone from which all the softer rock has been washed away. For the past thousand years, the arch has stood strong, but its fragility is echoed by the just-visible remains of former rocky structures dotted all along this section of the coast.

Following the sweeping curve of the bay, the rocky archway steps out into the waves. It's only a short swim from the shelving shingle beach out beneath the arch, but it's a real adventure. The water as far as the arch is relatively calm – if you take your goggles you might spot the schools of mackerel that gather in the sheltered bay – but passing through the arch and emerging into the open sea is an exhilarating experience.

Durdle Door sees around 200,000 visitors each year, so a swim is best done out of season or in the early morning or late on a summer evening to avoid the crowds. There are several options to make a longer adventure swim: once through the arch, you can continue along the coast eastwards, either coming in at St Oswald's Bay, making sure you swim clear of the rocks at Man O' War Cove, or carrying on past Stair Hole, with its arches and holes formed from Lulworth Crumple – the local 'folded' limestone – to reach the scallop shell-shaped Lulworth Cove. Caution: be aware of strong tidal pull and drifting. Do not jump from the arch as there is a submerged reef.

Challenge level: ✪✪✪✪✪ for beach to arch, higher for open-sea swim
Location: Durdle Door, Wareham, BH20 5 (approximate postcode)
OS grid ref: SY 805802
Distance: 330 feet (100m) from beach to arch
Map: OS Explorer OL15

Local Highlights

➡ Durdle Door Holiday Park is large and popular; however, it does have a tents-only area and is perfectly positioned for an early-morning swim.
➡ This section of coast is also great for exploring by kayak. Jurassic Coast Activities leads guided paddles here (www.jurassiccoastactivities.co.uk).
➡ Explore the atmospheric ruins of nearby Corfe Castle (National Trust).

18 Paddle Studland Bay ⊛ ⊛

The sheltered waters of Studland Bay make it a great spot for a relaxed paddle, whether you have your own boat or hire one. In calm weather the water's amazingly clear, and you can spot seaweed and crabs on the sandy seabed. There are swimming-only areas, ideal for first forays into sea swimming, but with a boat you can head further out and explore this fascinating part of the coast in more

collaboration between the Wildlife Trusts, the National Trust and Studland Sea School, costs £3 and is available from the Studland Sea School HQ on Middle Beach (www. studlandseaschool.co.uk) or the Studland National Trust shop. Kayak and paddleboard hire is available from Studland Watersports (www.studlandwatersports.co.uk) and guided kayaking, foraging, paddleboarding and snorkelling adventures can be booked through Fore/Adventure (www.foreadventure.co.uk).

Challenge level: ✪✪✪✪✪ **if staying within marked areas; up to** ✪✪✪✪✪ **if kayaking on open sea**
Location: Middle Beach, Studland Bay, Dorset, BH19 3AP
Map: OS Explorer OL15

detail. The sheltered bay offers relatively safe paddling but there are strong tides further out, so unless you're an experienced paddler stay well within the marked kayaking area, or join one of the many excellent guided expeditions out to the towering chalk turrets of Old Harry Rocks. There's also a Kayak Wildlife Trail around the bay that follows the coast through some of the best spots for seeing the local wildlife, including seabirds, seals and dolphins. The official guide, a

Local Highlights

→ Have an island adventure on Brownsea in Poole Harbour. Owned by the National Trust, this island is a wildlife reserve and a peaceful yet exciting place to explore. Day trips from Sandbanks/Poole. Holiday cottages/camping also available.
→ The section of coast path that runs around the headland at Old Harry Rocks is suitable for mountain bikes, so explore the area on two wheels, taking in Corfe Castle, the Purbeck Way and Nine Barrow Down, and the trails at Rempstone.
→ Stay at Burnbrake Campsite, near Corfe Castle.

19 Bikepack the Wessex Ridgeway

The Wessex Ridgeway Trail is an adventurous route that winds along Dorset's chalk ridge backbone from the Wiltshire border in the east to the Devon border in the west, with glorious views throughout. The majority of the route follows inviting trails along the grassy escarpment, but in places it drops down into secluded valleys and climbs over green, rounded hills. Each section of the trail has its own unique identity and delights to explore.

At 62 miles (100km) it's an inviting distance for an adventure too. The on-foot route starts at Ashmore on the Dorset/Wiltshire border and continues to Lyme Regis, whereas the cycling section is a couple of miles shorter, starting at the village of Tollard Royal and

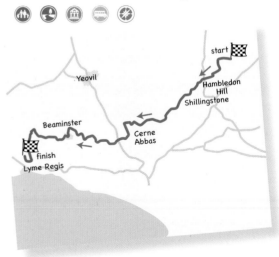

Challenge level: ✪✪✪✪✪
Start: Tollard Royal, Ashbourne, Dorset
OS grid ref: ST 943177
Finish: Champernhayes, Bridport, DT6 6DF
Distance: 62 miles/100km
Maps: OS Explorer 116, 117 and 118

41

ending in Champernhayes, just north of Lyme Regis. The route meanders through wildlife-filled chalk downland, climbs magnificent hillforts such as Hambledon Hill and crosses beautifully clear chalk streams. It passes through pretty villages such as Cerne Abbas and takes in stunning views of the Blackmore and Marshwood vales. The finish at the coast on the dramatic Dorset and East Devon World Heritage Site is a well-earned reward for having completed the journey. The route is waymarked throughout with a wyvern – a two-legged dragon associated with the ancient kingdom of Wessex.

Local Highlights

→ From the finish at Champernhayes, drop down into Lyme Regis for fossil hunting, exploring the beach and a walk along the historic harbour wall, known as the Cobb.
→ Explore the mountain biking trails in the woods at Shillingstone about halfway along the route (www.okefordhillbikepark.co.uk).
→ Camp at Hook Farm, a pretty, 20-minute walk up the river from Lyme Regis (hookfarmcamping.com).

Southern & Eastern England

There's a surprising wealth of outdoor adventure to be found in and around the nation's capital, from rolling chalk downland to large areas of deciduous woodland, and nearly half of London itself is green space. Further afield, the wild fens, sandy beaches and abundant wildlife of East Anglia are waiting to be explored.

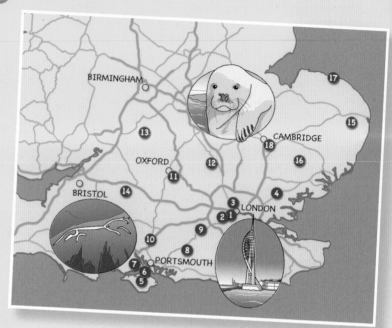

London & Essex

Escaping within London is all about the city's beautiful parks, from running or cycling the trails around Richmond Park and Wimbledon Common to a swim in Hyde Park's Serpentine.

The mighty – but busy – River Thames is a great place to explore by kayak or paddleboard, preferably with an experienced guide.

Outdoor adventures also abound east of London, on Essex's Chelmer and Blackwater Canal, in Epping Forest and on the National Trust-owned Northey Island.

South-East Coast & the Downs

South of London lie bustling towns and cities, picturesque countryside, rolling hills, dense forests and a long stretch of coastline offering opportunities for trail running, mountain biking and swimming. The South Downs National Park is a perfect weekend escape, while the Isle of Wight is definitely somewhere for those who love their adventures on two wheels.

The Chilterns & the Cotswolds

North-west of London, there's a wonderful remoteness about the long ridge of the Chilterns, etched with the white trails of the Ridgeway and the Icknield Way, and providing some wonderful places to explore, such as the National Trust's Ashridge Estate with its running and cycling trails.

Slightly further out, Oxfordshire's deep rivers wind through lush green landscapes and the Cotswold Way makes its 100-mile (161km) undulating journey through the rolling countryside.

East Anglia

East Anglia comprises Norfolk, Suffolk and Cambridgeshire and offers many glorious beaches, abundant opportunities to spot wildlife, and peaceful rivers to swim in or to explore in a canoe or on a paddleboard. The Norfolk and Suffolk Broads are a unique, wildlife-rich landscape networked by navigable lakes and rivers.

Escape the city by bike

The Thames Valley Cycleway starts at Putney Bridge in south-west London and makes its way along a mixture of riverside paths, quiet lanes, bridleways and purpose-built cycleways to Oxford, an interesting and enjoyable adventure of just under 100 miles (161km). Unlike the Thames Path National Trail, which is for walkers only, it only follows the general direction of the river – you can't cycle alongside the river all the way to Oxford. The route follows the Sustrans National Cycle Network Routes 4 and 5 and is well waymarked throughout. There are some stretches of multi-user track alongside fairly busy roads, but in general the route does an excellent job of avoiding these and the cycling is enjoyable and interesting. Of its 99 miles (159km), approximately 40 (64km) are traffic-free.

The route: starting at Putney Bridge, the route follows the river and heads through Richmond Park, before leaving London towards Staines. From here it leaves the waterside, with only the occasional glimpse of the Thames until it reaches Oxford. On the way it passes through Windsor Great Park before arriving in Reading. Between Reading and Wallingford there's some lovely cycling on quiet country lanes, and also some challenging climbs as you go up and over the Chilterns. After Wallingford it's a fairly straightforward ride via Abingdon to finish at Oxford. There's a wide range of refreshment and accommodation options along the route, and the time you take will depend on the level of challenge you're after.

Challenge level: ✪✪✪✩✩
Start: Putney Bridge, London, SW15 2PD
Finish: central Oxford
Distance: 99 miles/159km
Maps: National Cycle Network Route 4 and Route 5, Sustrans OS Explorer 160, 161, 170, 171, 172 and 180

Local Highlights

➡ For a longer, multi-day ride NCN Route 4 joins the Kennet and Avon cycle route to Bristol and South Wales (see page 37).
➡ Take some time out to explore the Chilterns as the route passes through the hills and the Vale of the White Horse.

44

A run around Richmond Park always has a surprise in store, whether you're heading out on a frosty, misty morning through smart coffee-scented streets, or joining a group for a sunny, social Sunday-morning run. It's so near to the city, yet some reaches have a wild feel that's more akin to moorland or meadow. Hills rise to a tree-lined horizon; herds of red and fallow deer graze peacefully in the shade or lie in big groups in the grass; ducks and geese waddle about the ponds. Created by Charles I as a deer park in the 17th century, Richmond is the largest of London's Royal Parks. It is internationally important as a wildlife conservation area and is also a National Nature Reserve, a Site of Special Scientific Interest and a Special Area of Conservation.

The Tamsin Trail is a great introduction to running in Richmond, and our go-to route whenever we're in the city. It's a waymarked, surfaced loop around the edge of the park, ideal for a gentle jog or a hard training session, or even for a timed 6-mile (10km) with a mile's warm-up. The loop is buggy- and wheelchair-friendly and is also perfect for exploring as you can leave and join it as you wish, following the smaller trails into the heart of the park. It's worth getting there early in the summer months to avoid the crowds.

Challenge level: ★☆☆☆☆
Start/finish: Pembroke Lodge, Richmond, TW10 5HX
Distance: 7¼ miles/11.7km
Map: OS Explorer 161

Local Highlights

→ Explore the park by bike. Park Cycle (www.parkcycle.co.uk) has a range of bikes to hire, including kids' bikes, seats and tagalongs.
→ Refuel at the Roehampton Café, or at one of the refreshment points located near Broomfield Hill and Pen Pond car parks.
→ Wander around the 40-acre Isabella Plantation, a Victorian woodland with streams, ponds, fascinating wildlife and the national collection of 'Wilson's Fifty' Kurume azaleas, imported from Japan in the 1920s.

3 Swim at Hampstead Heath Ponds

Set within the green oasis of north-west London's Hampstead Heath are 30 or so spring-fed ponds that were originally dug in the 17th and 18th centuries as reservoirs. Three of these are now large freshwater swimming ponds – one for women, one for men and one mixed. The ponds are open for year-round swimming, within specified opening times, and are lifeguard-patrolled. Swimwear is compulsory, and you are permitted to wear a triathlon or swimming wetsuit at the lifeguard's discretion. There are changing areas, benches and pegs for belongings, toilets and showers, along with sunbathing areas.

The water in the ponds is brown and murky, but the quality is regularly monitored and there's plenty of wildlife, including kingfishers, herons and crayfish. The ponds are very deep, with access via ladders, so you do need to be a confident swimmer.

The ponds are managed by the City of London Corporation, which asks for a voluntary entry fee of £1–£2 towards the maintenance of the pools and facilities.

During the summer months the water temperature can reach a balmy 20+ degrees Celsius; however, for the ultimate challenge head to the ponds in winter, when it can be near zero.

Local Highlights

→ Explore the area around Hampstead Heath's tumulus, nearly 800 acres of ancient heathland and woodland.

→ Eat at the Castle Café in Stoke Newington, part of the famous Castle climbing centre – one of the best indoor climbing venues in London

→ Hire a traditional Thames skiff – a wooden rowing boat – and camp out on the river (www.skiffhire.com).

Challenge level: ⭐⭐○○○
Location: Hampstead Heath, Highgate, London, NW3 1BP
Map: OS Explorer 173

4 The Chelmer & Blackwater Canoe Trail

The river Chelmer rises in Debden in the north-west of Essex and flows south to Chelmsford. Here it becomes a canal, continuing east to join the canalised section of the river Blackwater. Engineered by John Rennie between 1793 and 1797, it is the only waterway in the country that is still owned and operated by its original company of proprietors. The river was straightened in the early 19th century to make it more navigable for boats carrying coal and timber – in one case by moving an island, clearly visible on a 1777 map, to fill in a bend. Today it's a pretty place, the riverbanks lined with willows and the former industrial buildings, such as Papermill Lock, turned into refreshment stops. The route is almost entirely rural, with just a short industrial section through Heybridge village. You will need a licence to paddle the main river – a day licence (£5 at the time of writing) is available to buy online from waterways.org.uk.

The full route is approximately 14 miles (22.5km) long, with 11 locks. Papermill Lock, halfway along, has a tearoom and many moored boats and interesting buildings – a paddle from here to Hoe Mill and back makes for a shorter alternative of around 5 miles (8km) with only one portage.

Further on, at Beeleigh, the river Blackwater and the top of the tideway form a confluence. After this the Long Pond carries the Chelmer and Blackwater Navigation down the final stretch to Heybridge Basin, where there are plenty of waterside pubs for post-paddle refreshments.

Challenge level: ✪✪✪✪✪
Start: Springfield Lock, Wharf Road Car Park, CM2 6HY – put in just below the lock
OS grid ref: TL 717063
Finish: Daisy Meadow car park, Heybridge Basin, Maldon
OS grid ref: TL 871069
Distance: 14 miles/22.5km (11 locks)
Maps: OS Explorer 176 and 183

Local Highlights

→ Enjoy a Tiptree cream tea at The Lock tearoom, owned by the makers of Tiptree preserves.

→ Explore Northey Island, owned by the National Trust and the closest you'll find to wilderness in Essex. It only becomes an island at high tide, so time your walk carefully.

→ Sleep on Northey Island – the annual summer Castaway weekend gives you the opportunity to stay on the island, with plenty of entertainment provided for all the family.

47

5 The Tennyson Trail

Outside its busy cities, Hampshire encompasses some wonderful areas of wildness in which to seek out adventures, including the western part of the South Downs National Park, the southern edge of the North Wessex Downs AONB and the majority of the New Forest.

As well as being a great place for cycling, the Isle of Wight has a strong running heritage, hosting the oldest continuously held marathon, which has been run here every year since 1957. The many trails that cover the island make for some truly great running, with beautiful views, varied landscapes and lots of wildlife to spot – this is one of the few remaining areas in the UK to have a thriving population of red squirrels. The Tennyson Trail is a challenging, scenic run across the Isle of Wight, starting from Carisbrooke in the island's centre and heading out over hills and through picturesque Brighstone Forest to the Needles and around to Alum Bay. The route climbs over Bowcombe Down, Brighstone Down,

Mottistone Down, Compton Down, Tennyson Down and High Down, each with its own tough ascent and fast descent. The fantastic central ridge has great views across the island and out to sea. Finally, the route descends to its finish at Alum Bay. If you're keen to complete a full crossing of the island there are a number of enjoyable options. One of the best starts in Ryde and follows the Nunwell Trail south and then the Bembridge Trail west to Newport, winding through the streets to Carisbrooke, where you can pick up the Tennyson Trail to Freshwater to complete a full north–south crossing.

Local Highlights

➡ Refuel at The Hut at Colwell Bay, Freshwater. On a calm day the swimming in the bay is fantastic.
➡ Take part in the annual Solent Swim: 1.2 miles (1.9km) from Hurst Castle on the mainland to Colwell Bay on the Isle of Wight.

Challenge level: ●●●○○
Start: Carisbrooke, Newport, PO30 1NR
Finish: Alum Bay, PO39 0JD
Distance: 14½ miles/23km
Map: OS Explorer OL29

The Isle of Wight has been called one of the best places to cycle in the world. Arriving here on one of the many ferries from the mainland, it's easy to see why. A network of beautifully maintained tracks, byways and bridleways criss-crosses the island, linking the main settlements through varied and interesting countryside.

The Round the Island cycle route is 62 miles (exactly 100km) long and is well-waymarked with blue and white signs. It's all on road, but the roads are generally very quiet, many running close to the coast with great views out to sea. The route is undulating and can be exposed and windy at times, though most cyclists should expect to complete the loop in a day. If you want to explore more along the way, however, there's a huge range of places to stay, allowing you to split it up into two or more sections. There are also plenty of places to stop for refreshment en route, particularly in the larger villages and towns, including Cowes and East Cowes, Ventnor and Yarmouth, together with Freshwater, Bembridge, Niton and Brighstone. You can cycle the route clockwise or anticlockwise, starting and finishing in Cowes and crossing over the floating bridge to finish.

49

Local Highlights

→ If you'd rather not cycle the route alone, join 3,000 others during the Isle of Wight Randonnee, a non-competitive cycle ride that takes place every spring.
→ The Isle of Wight Cycle Festival, a week-long celebration of all things cycling, is held each September, and is another fantastic way to experience the island by bike.
→ Wake up to spectacular coastal views camping at Grange Farm in Brighstone Bay (www.grangefarmholidays.com).

Challenge level: ★★★☆☆
Start/finish: Cowes, Isle of Wight
Distance: 62 miles/100km
Map: OS Explorer OL29

7 A Beaulieu River swim

The Beaulieu River was once known as the river Exe and runs for 12 miles (19km) from Lyndhurst in the New Forest to the sea on Hampshire's coast at Needs Ore Point. The final 4 miles (6.4km) of the river, downstream from the village of Beaulieu, are tidal and make for a challenging but enjoyable swim. Begin your swim as the tide starts to fall, following the wide twists and turns seawards – it's a delightful experience, a real feeling of adventure with plenty to see along the way. The Beaulieu River and its bank form part of a National Nature Reserve, particularly important for its bird life. Needs Ore Point is home to the largest colony of black-headed gulls in the country, and further upstream you might spot Brent geese, teal, ringed plover, black-tailed godwit, terns, shelduck, curlew, redshank and oyster catchers.

Avoid swimming here after heavy rain or during extremes of tide; note also that swimming is prohibited in the marinas, so enter the water well away from them. Be aware of the many boats that use this stretch of water – a bright swimming cap and a safety buoy are strongly recommended. The picturesque Solent Way runs alongside the river as far as the historical shipbuilding village of Buckler's Hard; if you jump out here, again taking care to avoid the marina, it's a pleasant route back to Beaulieu.

Challenge level: ✪✪✪✪✪
Start: Beaulieu village, SO42 7YG
Finish: Buckler's Hard, SO42 7XB
Distance: 2½ miles/4km
Map: OS Explorer OL22

Local Highlights

→ Take part in an organised open-water swimming session at nearby Ellingham Lake: Wednesday and Saturday mornings, 6–8 a.m. (there is an entry fee).
→ Go exploring in the New Forest, where you'll find miles of walking, running and cycling trails, wild ponies and diverse landscapes from forest and heathland to the picturesque coastline that edges Lepe Country Park.

8 Black Down & the Temple of the Winds 🏞️ 💧 🏛️

At 920 feet (280m), Black Down marks the summit of the South Downs National Park. It's a place that feels elevated and remote from its surroundings, and here and there from the paths that circle the hills are glimpses of far-reaching views of the towns and countryside below. Scots pines grow tall and straight, and belted Galloway cattle – part of a conservation grazing programme – roam the hillsides. Black Down has a fascinating history, with flint artefacts suggesting there has been human habitation here since the Mesolithic period, some 8,000 years ago. The area is also home to Aldworth, built in 1869 by Alfred Lord Tennyson. At the southern tip of the loop you'll find the Temple of the Winds, a place to stop and take in the magnificent views. The seat here is in memory of the Hunter family, who gave Black Down to the National Trust in 1944, and Tennyson's old summerhouse stood near here.

The route: from the start it's about a mile (1.6km) up and along the main ridge, heading due south on a sunken track edged with bilberries in summer. There are several paths, all of which wind enjoyably in a north–south direction to eventually reach the viewpoint at the Temple of the Winds. The trig point marking the summit stands a couple of hundred metres north of the Temple of the Winds – a nice navigational challenge to find. Return by one of the many paths that lead back to the start.

Challenge level: ⭐✩✩✩✩
Start/finish: Tennyson's Lane main National Trust car park, Haslemere, GU27 3BJ
OS grid ref: SU 917311
Distance: 2 miles/3.2km
Map: OS Explorer OL33

9 Kayak the Wey Navigation

The Wey Navigation is Surrey's oldest waterway, running from Weybridge, at the River Thames, to Guildford 16 miles (26km) south. Here it joins the Godalming Navigation, extending the waterway another 4 miles (6.4km) to Godalming. This beautiful stretch of river, owned and managed by the National Trust, is an incredibly peaceful place to explore by kayak, as it is buzzing with wildlife and at times feels a million miles from the busy south-east. Much of the farmland it runs through has no public access, so you'll find yourself paddling through deserted, quiet countryside with just the herons for company. You can launch from the Wey Kayak Club in Guildford and explore from there – Dapdune Wharf along the way is well worth investigation. The kayak club also offers training courses and social paddles. The 4 miles (6.4km) between Guildford and Godalming provide a perfect introduction to the river, or you can paddle the full length over a day or more; there are 14 well-spaced locks and two sets of floodgates along the 20-mile (32km) stretch, so you'll need to be happy to portage these, along with any weirs you encounter.

To paddle here, you will need either a current Navigations Licence from the National Trust or British Canoeing membership. You can purchase a licence from the Navigations Office at Dapdune Wharf, where you can also get advice on current conditions. Avoid the river when it's in flood and be aware of other river users.

Challenge level: ★★★☆☆
Start: Wey Kayak Club, Guildford Waterside Centre, Riverside, Guildford, GU1 1LW
Finish: Godalming
Distance: 4 miles/6.4km
Map: OS Explorer 145

Local Highlights

➡ Camp at Mellow Farm at the edge of the Wey near Farnham. There are lots of adventures available to those staying on site; you can hire a kayak or launch your own from the site (mellowfarmadventure.co.uk).
➡ Don't miss the Wey River Festival, with food, crafts and an illuminated floating pageant, held each September (free entry).
➡ Refuel or stay at the Merry Harriers in Hambledon, just outside Godalming, or go on a llama tour there (www.merryharriers.com).

10 Bikepack the South Downs Way

The South Downs Way National Trail runs along a chalk ridge through the heart of the National Park, a 100-mile (160km) adventure designed for walkers/runners, cyclists and horse riders. It's one of the great long-distance challenges in the UK, with railway stations at either end and plenty of campsites along the way, meaning you can break up the trip as you wish. At the time of writing the fastest time for a cyclist is 7 hours 50 minutes, and the fastest there-and-back time is 17 hours 47 minutes – but how long you take to enjoy the experience is up to you. The route is well waymarked, following the blue arrows that designate the bridleway – but be aware that this does at times differ from the walking route. There's an excellent printable leaflet on mountain biking the South Downs Way produced by National Trail that details the bike repair and hire shops, water taps and railway stations along the route. There's much to see on the route, including startlingly clear and internationally important chalk rivers, rare chalk grasslands and beautiful ancient woodland. The trail passes through or by five National Nature Reserves and dozens of Sites of Special Scientific Interest.

Challenge level: up to ★★★★★ if done in one go
Start: Winchester Cathedral, SO23 9LS
Finish: Grand Parade, Eastbourne, BN21 3YL
Distance: 100 miles/161km
Maps: OS Explorer OL3, OL8, OL10, OL11, OL25 and OL32

Local Highlights

→ There are many campsites along the South Downs Way; however, a couple of our favourites are the intriguing Sustainability Centre in East Meon (www.sustainability-centre.org) and Housedean Farm in Lewes (www.housedean.co.uk), both of which are right on the route. Or there's Blackberry Wood campsite near Ditchling, where you'll find an incredible range of glamping options, from treehouses to helicopters.
→ If you're not in a rush and not going for a record time, there are lots of wonderful places to explore along the Way. Try Arundel Castle, Arundel Wetlands Centre and Swanbourne Lake, or Butser Hill – the highest point on the route – and nearby Queen Elizabeth Country Park.

Local Highlights

➡ Two popular pubs, the Trout and the Perch – one at each end of Port Meadow – are perfect for a post-swim pint.
➡ Camp at Barefoot Camping at Northmoor Lock, a few miles upstream of Port Meadow. There's direct access to the river for swimming, boating and paddling – you could even arrive by boat.
➡ Explore the Chiswell Valley – locally known as Happy Valley – following boardwalks through a wild sweep of reed bed, fen and ancient wet woodland. Look out for wild orchids and circling birds of prey.

  Not long ago, swimming in the Thames might not have sounded like an appealing prospect. A 1957 survey of the river in London found eels to be the only sign of life. Today, however, the Thames is home to over 120 species of fish and popular swimming spots are emerging along its length – although swimming is prohibited in the city stretch because of strong currents and numerous boats. In 2006, Lewis Pugh swam the whole river, from its source in the Cotswolds to the sea, although severe drought at the time meant the 350km route took 21 days – twice as long as he'd planned.

One of the best places to sample the delights of swimming the Thames is in rural Oxfordshire. The stretch alongside Port Meadow, from Godstow Lock to Danger Bridge, is a perfect introduction. Port Meadow is Oxford's oldest monument, with a long history of human use from burial to horse racing. It is common land with grazing rights – there's a resident herd of ponies – and important for its rare collection of wild plants. It was while rowing up this stretch of the Thames that Lewis Carroll was inspired to write *Alice's Adventures in Wonderland*.

Don't attempt to swim during extremes of low or high water, and be aware of boat traffic and submerged roots and weeds.

Challenge level: ⭐⭐⭐⭐⭐
Start: just below Godstow Lock
OS grid ref: SP 485089
Finish: Danger Bridge
OS grid ref: SP 498073
Distance: 1½ miles/2.5km
Map: OS Explorer 1

12 Climb Ivinghoe Beacon

The trig point on the top of Ivinghoe Beacon stands 817 feet (249m) high at the northern end of the Chiltern Hills. Although some way short of the highest point, its prominent shape, position and location make visiting it a great adventure. The beacon is also the start (or the finish, if you're travelling the other way) of both the Ridgeway and the Icknield Way National Trails. It's hard to pinpoint exactly what it is about the place, but when you're there it somehow feels worthy of this honour – the beginning or the destination of a long journey, with either the anticipation or the memories of the adventures along the way. The annual Ridgeway Challenge begins here and sees runners tackling the full 86 miles (138km) to Avebury – it's one of the classic ultramarathons and a big tick on any ultrarunner's list.

There are a number of ways to ascend to the top of Ivinghoe Beacon; one of the most straightforward is to park at the NT Ivinghoe Beacon car park, just off the B489, and walk to the summit from there. The beacon is a grand place to watch sunrise, sunset, or both, so here you're perfectly placed to make an ascent when the weather is right. Another way is to begin at the Visitor Centre on the National Trust's Ashridge Estate (HP4 1LT – 2 miles (3.2km) from Tring Station) and head north along trails through the woods before ascending to the open ridge for the final stretch to the summit – about a 6-mile (10km) round trip.

Challenge Level: ★☆☆☆☆
Location: Ivinghoe Beacon, Aylesbury Vale, Dunstable, LU6 2EG
OS grid ref: SP 960168
Map: OS Explorer 181

55

Local Highlights

→ For 24-hour views and easy access to the beacon, camp at Town Farm campsite, just across the B489 (www.townfarmcamping.co.uk).
→ Explore the beautiful Ashridge Estate – the waymarked 16-mile (26km) Boundary Trail is a fantastic longer walk or run and is the route of an annual race (ashridgeboundaryrun.co.uk).
→ Sit outside at Brownlow Café on the estate and enjoy coffee and views, or picnic in the park.

13 The Cotswold Way

One of the many joys of exploring Britain's National Trails lies in the journeys they take you on. Each one is special, filled with interesting things to discover from historical sites to fascinating geological features, together with a unique mix of flora and fauna. Their preservation makes them special too – all have been worn into the landscape over thousands of years as the best way to travel through the region, whether that's because they are on high ground affording good visibility or on firm ground to avoid treacherous bogs and marshes, or because they provide a link between important places.

The 102-mile-long (164km) Cotswold Way, from Chipping Campden to Bath, lends itself well to walking and running adventures, not least because most of it isn't suitable for any means of transport other than two feet. You do not, of course, have to tackle it all in one go, although people do, either as an attempt

(www.racetothetower.co.uk) covers 53 miles (85km), finishing at Broadway Tower, or you could take on the full 102 miles (164km) by doing the Cotswold Way Century (www.cotswoldrunning.co.uk).

at the Fastest Known Time (20 hours 36 minutes at the time of writing) or as part of one of the races that take place here. But it's a length that lends itself well to a series of weekend expeditions, or to a week-long assault. You could bivvy along the route, camp at the campsites along the way, or stay in B&Bs for a welcome hot bath at the end of a long day. If you'd prefer company and aid stations along the way, you can take part in a fully supported event. Threshold Sport's Heineken Race to the Tower

Local Highlights
→ There's a wealth of fascinating history along the Cotswold Way, including the Neolithic burial chamber at Belas Knap and Sudeley Castle near Winchcombe. Or climb to the highest point on the trail: Cleeve Hill at 1,080 feet (330m).
→ The trail ends right in the heart of the city of Bath, a World Heritage Site. Explore the Roman Baths or head for the hills following the 10km Bath Skyline around the city's high, green spaces.

Challenge level: ✪✪✪✪✪
Start: Chipping Campden, GL55 6HB
Finish: Bath Abbey, BA1 1LT
Distance: 102 miles/164km
Maps: OS Explorer OL45, 155, 167, 168 and 179

14 Ride the Ridgeway

The Ridgeway National Trail runs for 87 miles (140km) from the World Heritage Site of Avebury in Wiltshire through the North Wessex Downs to finish at Ivinghoe Beacon in the Chilterns. As Britain's oldest road, it often traverses stretches of remote high ground, used over thousands of years by travellers, soldiers and herdsmen. The western half of the Ridgeway is an outstanding mountain bike trek, with 43 miles (69km) of mostly traffic-free riding through rolling chalk downland. It's a ride through history too, beginning at Avebury stone circle and passing many fascinating archaeological sites, including Stone Age and Bronze Age barrows, Iron Age hillforts and giant white horses carved into the chalk hillsides.

From the nearest station at Pewsey it's a pleasant hour's cycle along National Cycle Network Route 45 to the start of the Ridgeway at Avebury. From here the route is well waymarked, heading east on chalk tracks, grassy trails and quiet paths, with glorious views from the high points and very little road. The finish at Streatley is also well connected, with Goring and Streatley station just over the Thames bridge. The route is undulating, but there are few steep climbs and nothing too technical on the ground, so it's very achievable for anyone with a reasonable level of cycling experience, but still an engaging ride for the seasoned off-roader.

Challenge level: ✪✪✪✪✪
**Start: Avebury, Marlborough, SN8 1RF
(or Pewsey station, SN9 5EL)
Finish: Goring and Streatley station, Goring,
Reading, RG8 0ES
Distance: 43 miles/69km (+12 miles/19km
from Pewsey)
Maps: OS Explorer 157, 169 and 170**

Local Highlights

➡ Exploring the Ridgeway on foot is also an incredible experience. If you'd prefer some support along the way you can run all 86 miles (138km) as part of the annual Ridgeway Challenge, held in August each year, or the final 100km from Lewknor to Avebury at Race to the Stones, held in July.

➡ Take some time to explore the incredible megaliths at Avebury, a World Heritage Site with three stone circles, including the largest in Europe.

57

15 Swim around Outney Common

a wide loop around Outney Common is a perfect place to escape the heat of a summer's day. It's a real frog's-eye-view adventure, to use Deakin's words, with the river's looping course meaning there's always another corner to round, a new scene to discover, with cows watching lazily from the riverbanks, damselflies and dragonflies droning overhead and the high banks alive with wildlife. Start and finish at the northern tip of the Suffolk market town of Bungay, floating under the A143 before leaving its busy hum far behind.

Local Highlights

➡ Tackle the great mountain bike trails at Thetford Forest – there's something for everyone, from the 10km family ride to the 10-mile-long (16km) black route for experienced riders.

➡ This stretch of river is also great for kayaking – camp at Outney Meadow Campsite, where you can also hire boats (www.outneymeadow.co.uk).

The river Waveney forms the county boundary between Norfolk and Suffolk, running nearly 60 miles (97km) from Redgrave in the west, through the wildlife-rich Broads, to Lowestoft in the east, where it empties into the North Sea. A favourite spot of Roger Deakin, the founder of the wild swimming movement, the co-founder of the environmental charity Common Ground and the author of the masterpiece *Waterlog*, the two-mile (3.2km) stretch of the Waveney that makes its way in

Challenge level: ★★★☆☆
Start/finish: Outney Common, Bungay, Suffolk, NR35 1DS
Distance: 2 miles/3.2km
Map: OS Explorer OL40

16 Kayak the River Stour

The River Stour Navigation is one of the oldest navigations in the country and runs between Brundon Mill near Sudbury in Suffolk and Cattawade in Essex. With well-spaced locks and weirs to manage the water levels, there's no current and the whole stretch is an enjoyable and straightforward paddle through leafy Constable country – and in fact Constable loved to paint the goings-on here. The Environment Agency is the navigation

distance there are many shorter options, with a popular paddle being the 7 miles (11km) from Sudbury to Bures.

Challenge level: ✪✪✪✩✩
Start: Brundon Mill, Sudbury, CO10 1XR
Finish: Cattawade Barrier, Manningtree
OS grid ref: TM 100 331
Distance: 24½ miles/39.4km
Maps: OS Explorer 196 and 197

59

authority for this section of the river, and unless you have current British Canoeing membership, you'll need to acquire a licence from the agency (www.environment-agency. gov.uk) or from the River Stour Trust (www. riverstourtrust.org). At the time of writing, fees are £8.50 for a week's licence.

The full navigation, from Sudbury to the Cattawade Barrier at the exit to the North Sea, is a little under 25 miles (40km), but can be done in a day during the summer – a fantastic adventure, with easily managed portages and plenty of interesting places to explore and to refuel at along the way. There are three locks – Great Cornard lock, Dedham lock and Flatford lock – and 16 weirs. There's an annual organised Sudbury-to-the-Sea event – the S2C – which takes place in September. If you don't fancy the full

Local Highlights

→ Take afternoon tea at The Granary in Sudbury (open Easter to October), run by volunteers, with proceeds going to the River Stour Trust.
→ Hire a boat from Sudbury (www. outdoorhirecentres.com) or go on a guided canoe camping trip (www.riverstourboating. co.uk).
→ Camp by the river at Rushbanks Farm, CO6 4NA.

Local Highlights

→ Camp at the pretty, petite site at Scaldbeck Cottage in Morston or glamp at Amber's Bell Tents, Wiverton Hall, to be within morning running distance of the sea...

→ Explore the Peddar's Way and the Norfolk Coast Path, which combine to make a glorious 93-mile (150km) waymarked trail around this section of the country.

The 2-mile (3.2km) stretch of shingle beach at Cley on the north Norfolk coast is one of the best spots in the area for endurance swimming. Unlike most of the coast here it shelves steeply, so you can swim in deep water very close to the shore – but still be aware of strong currents, especially if you venture further out.

A visit to Cley isn't just about swimming – this is also an incredible place for wildlife. The marshes here are Norfolk Wildlife Trust's oldest nature reserve and are carefully managed, providing a blueprint for nature conservation across the country. The shingle beach and saline lagoons, along with the grazing marsh and reedbed, support large numbers of wintering and migrating wildfowl and waders; if you're lucky you might spot bitterns, marsh harriers and bearded tits. There's an eco-friendly visitor centre with a café, a shop and viewing areas (including viewing from a camera on the reserve), and the views from the visitor centre across the marsh to the sea are breathtaking.

Blakeney Point, just west of Cley, is a well-known seal-spotting venue and there are both common and Atlantic grey seal colonies here. There are several companies that run seal spotting trips out around the point, or you can make the 7-mile (11km) round trip on foot from the Norfolk Wildlife Trust car park at Cley Beach.

Challenge level: ✪✪✪✩✩ **for the sea swim – note that this swim is for experienced open-water swimmers only**
Location: Cley beach, Cley-next-the-Sea, Norfolk, NR25 7RZ
OS grid ref: TG 048453
Map: OS Explorer 251

18 Cambridge to Wicken Fen ride & wild camp

The result of an inspired joint venture between Sustrans and the National Trust, this enjoyable cycle route links Cambridge and neighbouring towns with the Trust's oldest nature reserve at Wicken Fen so that more people can enjoy the area without having to bring a car. The route starts in the bustling heart of Cambridge, whose university was founded in the 13th century, and escapes the city following waterside paths, traffic-free trails and quiet country lanes all the way to Wicken Fen. The National Trust has camping lodges at Wicken, where you can sleep in an open-fronted, covered lodge and experience night time at the reserve. You can book all four lodges for around £40, though early booking is advised.

The route: from central Cambridge follow NCN Route 11 along the southern bank of the river Cam. At Logan's Meadow, leave Route 11 and join NCN Route 51, continuing along the Cam through Stourbridge Common and Ditton Meadows. Continue on Route 51 all the way to Bottisham, where you'll find another branch of NCN Route 11 – the Lodes Way. Follow this enjoyable route through the countryside, riding through wild and windswept fens and passing Anglesey Abbey to reach Wicken Fen. Camp here, or enjoy a couple of hours' exploring before returning to Cambridge the same way.

Challenge level:
Start: Cambridge railway station, CB1 2JW
Finish: Wicken Fen Nature Reserve, Lode Ln, Wicken, Ely, CB7 5XP
Distance: 18 miles/29km each way
Maps: OS Explorer 209 and 226

Local Highlights

→ Take some time out to explore Wicken Fen itself, a 785-acre site of unique, wildlife-rich lowland. There's a wind pump and the original fenworkers' cottages to see, along with 9,000 species of wildlife including rare bitterns and the more recent additions of Highland cattle and Eastern European Konik ponies.
→ See the reserve from the water on board the *Mayfly*, an electric passenger ferry run by the National Trust (chargeable).

61

Central England

Aside from its busy cities and large-scale industry, England's central belt is also home to some of the most accessible, enjoyable outdoor adventure spots in the country. The Peak District, Britain's first National Park, is filled with high moors and technical trails for all kinds of outdoor adventures. There's also superb swimming and kayaking on the River Wye in Herefordshire and tough mountain bike challenges in the Malvern Hills.

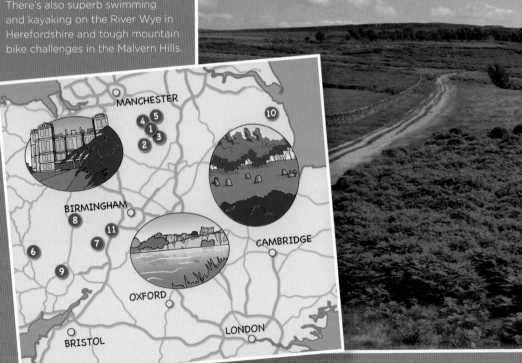

MANCHESTER

4 5
1 3
2

10

BIRMINGHAM

8

7 11

6

9

CAMBRIDGE

OXFORD

BRISTOL

LONDON

The Peak District

The Peak District National Park is split naturally into two halves – the Dark Peak to the north and the White Peak to the south. In contrast to the highly accessible White Peak's round, green limestone hills, dry valleys, runnable trails and craggy outcrops, the Dark Peak lies on millstone grit, with higher plateaus, wetter ground and wild moorland. It's hard to come to the Peak District and not feel moved to go adventuring: the White Peak has seemingly endless trails to run as well as an abundance of long-distance footpaths, and its clear rivers are perfect for kayaking and swimming. The landscape of the Dark Peak includes the long, stepped, gritstone edges for which the area is famous, particularly with rock climbers. Fell-running races are also an important annual event for most villages in the Peak District, with the young and old showing up of a weekend to battle with the hills. The Peak District is highly accessible, the Hope Valley railway passing right through, a direct link from Manchester and Sheffield.

The Midlands & the Welsh Borders

The Midlands is a place of great contrasts – and great adventures. Running roughly along the 177-mile (285km) Offa's Dyke Path, the border between England and Wales takes in tumbling rapids and wide, deep stretches of the river Wye running past the atmospheric ruins of Tintern Abbey, together with the Black Mountains with their accessible climbs leading to airy and expansive vistas. The Shropshire Hills' varied landscape of rolling farmland, woods and river valleys is rich in wildlife and geology and ingrained with heritage. Further north lies the Dee Valley and the Pontcysyllte Aqueduct, the centre of a World Heritage Site. Sherwood Forest and the picturesque, yet underexplored, Lincolnshire Wolds lie to the east.

Ride the Monsal Trail

The Monsal Trail is a former railway line converted into a multi-user path by cycling charity Sustrans and opened to the public in 2011. The trail begins at the former railway station in the pretty town of Bakewell, and runs 8½ miles (13.7km) along the valley to Topley Pike near Buxton. It's a perfect

introductory ride for those just finding their wheels, as well as for families and anyone simply wanting a relaxed but fascinating ride surrounded by dramatic limestone scenery, through railway tunnels and across the much-photographed Headstone Viaduct. These features, alongside the towering crags at Chee Dale and the beautiful, rolling White Peak landscape of Monsal Dale, make it one of the most varied and spectacular leisure rides in the country. Bike hire is available at Monsal Trail Cycle Hire based at the Hassop station café, and at Blackwell Mill at the Buxton end of the trail. The café at Hassop station is a

nice stop for a post-ride refuel, or you can ride over the bridleway to Bakewell (take the first left through a gate when heading from Hassop station towards Great Longstone) and get a picnic from the deli or sample an original Bakewell pudding.

If you're after more technical riding, there are several excellent mountain bike loops that take in sections of the Monsal Trail, or for a longer ride, or a multi-day one, you can link with the Pennine Bridleway, Tissington Trail or the High Peak Trail.

Local Highlights

→ Don't miss the annual Alpkit Big Shakeout, a weekend celebration of all things outdoors and adventure based next to the Monsal Trail at Thornbridge Hall, Great Longstone.
→ Sample the local Thornbridge ales at the Packhorse Inn, Little Longstone, or at the brewery itself in Bakewell.
→ Visit Raven Tor in Miller's Dale, just off the Monsal Trail, a dramatic overhanging limestone crag that's home to some of the country's toughest rock-climbing routes.

Challenge level: ✪✪✩✩✩
Start: Bakewell station (disused), DE45 1BU
Finish: Topley Pike, Buxton, SK17 9TE
Distance: 8½ miles/13.7km
Map: OS Explorer OL24

2 Explore Thor's Cave

Thor's Cave, also known as Thyrsis's Cave, is a natural cavern located in the Manifold Valley, in the Staffordshire region of the White Peak. An ancient site of human habitation and burial, it's a popular spot for walkers and rock climbers. From the valley floor, the steep limestone crag soars upwards, with the gaping mouth of the cave visible, its opening at a height of around 260 feet (80m). Access to the cave is via a stepped path – about 200 steps in total – from the Manifold Way, but it is well worth the climb to explore its vast interior, striped with the colours of the different minerals, and the views out onto the valley below.

To find Thor's Cave, from the centre of Wetton village take the small road leading towards Wetton Mill and the Manifold Valley. As you leave the village, take the farm track to the left, signed to Thor's Cave. Alternatively, follow the Manifold Way as it runs along the river Manifold from Waterhouses all the way to the cave – and look out for kingfishers along the river.

Challenge level: ★★☆☆☆
Location: Thor's Cave, SK 098550
Start/finish: Wetton village, Staffordshire, DE6 2AF
OS grid ref: SK 109555
Distance: 6 miles/10km circular walk from Wetton
Map: OS Explorer OL24

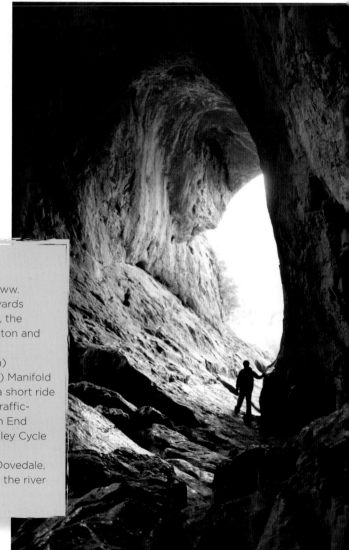

Local Highlights

→ Camp at Smithyfields Camping (www.smithyfieldscamping.com), just 100 yards (90m) from the excellent village pub, the George, and a few minutes from Wetton and Manifold villages.
→ Take a ride along the 13-mile (21km) Tissington Trail or the 9-mile (14.5km) Manifold Valley Cycle Trail, both of which are a short ride from the campsite, as well as being traffic-free. Bike hire is available from Brown End Farm Cycle Hire or from Manifold Valley Cycle Centre.
→ Visit nearby Ilam Park estate and Dovedale, and jump the stepping stones across the river Dove.

adventure too, with the simple aim of ticking off all nine of the edges in a day. The route is obvious for most of its length, following good paths along the tops of edges, though you will need to navigate some sections, and there are some boggy, unclear parts along the way. It is also possible to mountain bike the nine edges, although in many parts the route differs from the on-foot route.

Challenge level: ✪✪✪✪○
Start: Fairholmes
OS grid ref: SK 173894
Finish: Robin Hood Inn, Chesterfield Rd,
Baslow, Bakewell, DE45 1PQ
Distance: 20 miles/32km
Maps: OS Explorer OL1 and OL24

Edale Mountain Rescue Team, one of the busiest in the UK, covers the whole of the Peak District; the service is staffed entirely by volunteers and is run on charitable donations. Each September, the team organises a fundraising challenge: the Nine Edges Endurance. The event starts at Fairholmes, near Ladybower Reservoir, and traverses the 20 or so miles (32km) across the nine famous gritstone edges of Derwent, Stanage, Burbage North, Burbage South, Froggatt, Curbar, Baslow, Gardom's and Birchens, finishing at the Robin Hood Inn near Baslow. Your entry fee also buys you a pint at the pub. In the official event competitors have the option of running, walking or climbing (walkers and runners largely follow the same route, but climbers climb a route of their choice on each of the nine edges), with the fastest runners finishing in well under three hours. It is, however, a fantastic anytime

Local Highlights

➡ This part of the Peak District is famous for its gritstone bouldering – climbing without ropes on the lower rock formations. One of the best beginner-friendly bouldering venues is Burbage South, a sunny spread of easily accessed and friendly boulders below Burbage Edge.

➡ The shop and café in Hathersage is an institution in the outdoor world. Stock up on adventure guidebooks and refuel with a traditional Derbyshire oatcake.

➡ Local expert and running guide David Taylor offers guided runs and courses in the area (fellrunningguide.co.uk).

4 Scramble Crowden Clough

This classic Grade I scramble from the heart of the Hope Valley right up to very near the Peak District's highest point – Kinder Scout at 2,087 feet (636m) – makes for a great adventure, with several descent options. The best place to begin is at Edale station, joining the Pennine Way and following it east. At Upper Booth, turn right through a small gate, leaving the Pennine Way and following Crowden Brook. The upward route follows the brook the whole way, making this section very easy to navigate. Starting along a peaceful stretch through woodland, you'll soon find yourself in glorious Dark Peak countryside, walking along drystone-walled fields with the high fells rising on all sides. Further on, the trail becomes narrow and winding, criss-crossing the brook on rocky stepping stones, with always a good path to follow once you find it. As you ascend, the gradient steepens and large boulders provide some interesting but easy scrambling should you wish. After heavy rain there's plenty of water in the brook, enough for some pools that are deep enough for a dip in places. Rounding the final corner, the main scramble rears above, steep but manageable by most in the dry, but very slippery and tricky when the brook is in full flow. Any sections you don't fancy attempting can be bypassed using the trail on the left. Listen out for stonechats

Local Highlights

→ If you're confident in your navigation, try finding the true summit of Kinder Scout at 2,087 feet (636m) above sea level. It's north-east of the trig point at Kinder Low across trackless, boggy peat and marked only by a clump of grass near to a small pile of stones – but beware in poor visibility: many walkers find themselves lost and disorientated here. The National Trust has been working hard to restore the grassland on the plateau and the dams are fascinating to see.

clinking from the rocks and for the distinctive call of curlews, and watch peregrines and buzzards wheeling overhead.

Once you reach the summit on the Kinder Plateau, either scramble back down the way you came or turn left, following the top of the plateau west until you reach the Pennine Way – turn left on this and follow the classic descent of Jacob's Ladder back to Edale. Alternatively, turn right at the top of Crowden Clough and follow paths east to Grindsbrook Clough, an enjoyable and easier scramble in its own right that also provides an interesting descent taking you straight down into Edale.

Challenge level: ●●●●○
Start/finish: Edale station, Edale, Hope Valley, S33 7ZP
Distance: 7 miles/11.3km
Map: OS Explorer OL1

5 Ride around Ladybower

One of the classic Peak District mountain biking routes, this excellent, varied ride takes in a full loop of Ladybower Reservoir. It's a red- (medium-) graded ride, so you'll need to be a confident rider, but there's nothing too scary or technical out there. The route begins with a tough but enjoyable climb up and over Whinstone Lee Tor – the views from the top and the exhilarating descent more than make up for the effort involved in getting there. It finishes as it begins – in fine style – with a fantastic descent through woodland from Lockerbrook back down to Ladybower. At around 15 miles (24km), depending slightly on route choice, it's an awesome adventure, but even if you need to push it still won't take you all day.

The route: exiting Fairholmes car park, turn right at the roundabout and follow the path past the dam. Turn left onto a bridleway signed Footpath Derwent Edge. Continue straight on, climbing over Whinstone Lee Tor and sticking to the bridleway as it runs parallel to the A6013, descending to, and then following, the eastern shore of the reservoir, and taking to the cycleway along the main road.

Cross the reservoir at the dam and follow the Derwent Valley Heritage Way to Thornhill, turning right here and then right again in Aston where it is signed Win Hill and Hope Cross. As the road ends, continue on a bridleway north-west, passing Wooler Knoll and Hope Cross.

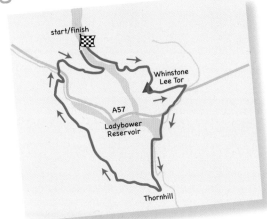

Cross straight over the main road and climb up through woodland before following the first obvious track down an exciting descent back to Fairholmes.

Challenge level: ✪✪✪✪✪
Start/finish: Fairholmes car park, S33 0AQ
Distance: 15 miles/24km
Map: OS Explorer OL1

69

Local Highlights

→ From the northernmost point of the reservoir follow the road north (park at Fairholmes as above), over a packhorse bridge to reach Slippery Stones at grid ref SK168950, a wonderful plunge pool, perfect for lazy summer afternoon adventures.
→ Climb the shapely, steep-sided Win Hill (1,519 feet/463m) just south of the reservoir for fantastic panoramic Peak District views.

6 Kayak the Wye 100 ⊕ 🏛

From Hay-on-Wye downstream to its meeting with the Severn Estuary at Chepstow, there has been a public right of navigation on the river Wye since the passing of an Act of Parliament in the late 17th century. By happy coincidence, this truly incredible stretch of river that runs along the Welsh borders through forest, rolling hills, towns and villages is 100 miles (161km) long: perfect for an adventure challenge. Depending on your preference, experience and time available, you can split the journey into distances you're happy paddling in one go, or across the days you have available. This is an area with such a wealth of history, wildlife and culture that even if you spend two weeks inching your way down the river you'll have plenty to discover at each stop along the way. There are plenty of places to stay, although much of the river bank is privately owned, so plan your stops carefully in advance. Please note that the final miles to Chepstow are tidal, and tides will have a big impact on paddling.

If you're not an experienced paddler, we'd advise either finishing your journey at Bigsweir Bridge near Llandogo (NP25 4TS) or going in the company of someone who knows the river.

If you don't fancy taking on the challenge alone, several companies run organised trips, with transport and accommodation included. Wye Canoes (www.wyecanoes.com), approved by British Canoeing, run a four-day trip with experienced guides and well-chosen stopovers, or there's hire available from Wye Valley Canoes (www.wyevalleycanoes.co.uk), where you'll also find the River Café and accommodation.

> *If you have never navigated the Wye, you have seen nothing*
>
> William Gilpin, 1782

Challenge level: ✪✪✪✪✪
Start: Glasbury, HR3 5NP
Finish: Chepstow, NP16 5EZ
Distance: 100 miles/161km
Maps: OS Explorer OL13, OL14, 189 and 201

Local Highlights

➡ Visit spectacular Symonds Yat for rock climbing, rapids and peregrine falcon watching.
➡ Camp at the Old Station campsite at Tintern, a simple, peaceful site and a perfect base for exploring the Wye Valley.

Local Highlights

→ Visit St Anne's Well – its water considered to have healing powers over the centuries – and refuel at the quirky St Anne's Well Café.
→ Recently reinvented after a long absence, the legendary Malvern Hills mountain bike festival is held at Eastnor Castle in June.

natural mineral springs and wells, which led to the development of Great Malvern as a spa town in the early 19th century. They are also famous for being the birthplace of composer Edward Elgar, who found inspiration for many of his works here.

The full traverse of the Malverns, from End Hill in the north to Chase End Hill in the south, is a great day out – though we'd suggest walking it over two days, or stepping up to the challenge of a there-and-back if you're running. From the summits of the two end hills the distance is around 9 miles (14.5km), ticking off all 15 major summits en route, but, depending on your transport options, you'll need to add at least a mile at each end. Taking cars is a logistical challenge, but possible – there's parking at North Hill car park, just north of the start, and at Hollybush, just north of the finish. It's doable by train too, although this adds a few miles or a taxi ride – Malvern Link is the closest station to the start and Ledbury is closest to the finish, or there's a YHA and camping at Hollybush if you want to make a weekend of it. CAUTION: there are several main road crossings on the route.

Formed from some of the most ancient rocks in England – around 680 million years old – the Malvern Hills run north–south for about 8 miles (13km) in between Great Malvern and the pretty village of Colwall. Looking east from the top of the ridge there are views across the flat lands of the river Severn valley, with the Cotswolds beyond. In wonderful contrast, to the west are the rolling hills of Herefordshire giving way to the Brecon Beacons. The highest point of the hills is Worcestershire Beacon at 1,395 feet (425m), but the most interestingly shaped is the Herefordshire Beacon, where the Iron Age hillfort known as the British Camp is clearly visible. The hills are famous for their

Challenge level: ✪✪✪✩✩
Start: End Hill
OS grid ref: SO 767469
Finish: Chase End Hill
OS grid ref: SO 761354
Distance: 9 miles/14.5km
Map: OS Explorer 190

8 The Long Mynd day out

The Shropshire Hills Area of Outstanding Natural Beauty (AONB) covers over 300 square miles (800 sq km) of south-west Shropshire, with a stretch along the Welsh borders. Within easy reach of many of the Midlands' towns and cities, it's a great place to escape to – and if you venture away from the more popular areas you'll find some properly wild and remote places, such as the aptly named Wild Moor. When we visited Long Mynd (meaning 'long mountain'), a dramatic, steep-edged plateau that runs 7 miles (11km) through the Shropshire Hills, we were seeking out the best adventure to include here; but we encountered a problem – there were just too many to choose from! This is a place that's designed for adventures – there's glorious, deep, permitted reservoir swimming at Carding Mill; there's Minton Batch, one of the best sections of mountain bike singletrack in the country; there are the views of Snowdonia from the summit of Brown Clee Hill which, at 1,790 feet (546m), is also the highest point in Shropshire; there's stunning Carding Mill

Local Highlights

→ The Shropshire Hills Mountain Bike and Outdoor Pursuit Centre (www.mtb-shropshire.co.uk) has bike hire, trail maps, a shop and a repairs centre.
→ Small Batch Camping (www.smallbatch-camping.co.uk) is positioned right in the heart of the hills, with trails leading from the site. It gets busy during peak times, but is an absolute gem when quiet.
→ Hire an expert guide to show you the best trails from Flattyres MTB (flattyres-mtb.co.uk).

Valley and the Bronze Age Bodbury Ring; and there's the long, beautiful section of trail that follows the Shropshire Way the full length of the Mynd. Best of all, you don't need a car, as Church Stretton railway station deposits you right in the centre of the action.

Challenge level: various
Location: Long Mynd, Church Stretton, Shropshire, SY6 6PG
OS grid ref: SO 455936
Map: OS Explorer 217

9 swim the Wye

Symonds Yat sits deep within the forested Wye Valley, straddling the counties of Herefordshire and Gloucestershire. There's a wealth of history here, including the bones of hyenas, sabre-toothed cats and a mammoth in and around the caves of the valley and evidence of 12,000 years of human habitation. One of the best river swims anywhere in the country has to be the wonderful 7½-mile-long stretch between Kerne Bridge and Huntsham Bridge, with plenty of opportunities to get out and explore the Wye Valley Walk that runs alongside the river. The Wye is also an excellent canoeing river, so look out for boats as you swim.

There are many other adventures to be found here too. The deep gorge cut into the carboniferous limestone by the river has exposed many impressive cliff faces, making this a popular climbing venue – and look out here for the resident peregrine falcons taking flight. In terms of canoeing, paddlers have rights of access between Hay-on-Wye and Chepstow. The Symonds Yat section is an important stretch for paddling and the short section of rapids next to the island is owned by British Canoeing to safeguard it for future paddlers.

Challenge level: ✪✪✪✪✪ **for swimming the full 7½ miles/12km**
Start: Kerne Bridge, Herefordshire, HR9 5QT
OS grid ref: SO 581189
Finish: Huntsham Bridge, HR9 7BX
OS grid ref: SO 567181
Distance: 7½ miles/12km
Map: OS Explorer OL14

Local Highlights

➡ The annual Wild Wye Swim is organised by the Severn Area Rescue Association (SARA), with 12km, 7km and 1km swimming events along this stretch of the river. Held in September, it's a great way to explore this beautiful stretch of the Wye with plenty of support, company and refreshments (wildwyeswim.org.uk).

10 The Lincs Wolds Way

The Lincolnshire Wolds is a range of hills classified as an Area of Outstanding Natural Beauty (AONB) that runs parallel to the North Sea coast between the river Humber in the north-west and the Lincolnshire Fens in the south-east. The chalk and limestone landscape makes for rolling grassy hills, farmland and steep, wide glacial valleys filled with wildflowers in summer. This is not a hilly region, however, and the highest point in the Wolds, and indeed in the whole of Lincolnshire, is Wolds Top, at just 168 m. Often forgotten by guidebooks, it's a delightful place to visit, with a vast network of footpaths and bridleways. To the east of the Wolds are sandy beaches where you can spot grey seal colonies.

The Lincs Wolds Way is a waymarked 76-mile (122km) circular route designed to take in the best of the Wolds and traversing the high ground wherever possible. Its creator, Tony Groom, suggests breaking the distance down into five stages for a comfortable six hours' walking a day; however, it is certainly an ideal route to try in three or even two days – or if you're looking for a real epic, in a oner. Tony is also a local walking guide and can help you explore the area; a detailed guide to walking the Lincs Wolds Way is also available on his website, www.lincswoldswalking.co.uk.

Because of its good transport links and great range of food and accommodation options, the route's suggested start/finish point is Louth, known as the 'Gateway to the Wolds'.

Challenge level: ✪✪✪✪✩
Start/finish: Navigation Warehouse, Louth, Lincolnshire
OS grid ref: TF 337879
Distance: 76 miles/120km
Maps: OS Explorer 273 and 282

74

Local Highlights

→ Lincolnshire is home to the largest collection of small-leaved lime woods in Britain. These stunning, ancient woodland areas are best visited when the trees are in leaf: bright green and fragrant in the spring and summer and ablaze with reds and golds in autumn. There are many trails for walking, running and cycling through the woods – a perfect way to explore.

11 The Four Stones at Clent ⚇ 🏛

Just 10 miles (16km) south-west of the city of Birmingham rise the Clent Hills, a wonderfully peaceful place to escape to, as long as you visit outside busy times. There's a great network of footpaths, bridleways and trails that invite exploration – climb to the top of the ridge on a clear day and you'll be rewarded with great views over the Cotswolds, the Shropshire Hills and the Welsh borders, as well as over the surrounding urban areas. There's something particularly special about dusk on the hills, a feeling of being removed from it all, looking down on the city lights twinkling far below. In the early summer, bluebells carpet the woodland floor, and Walton Hill, the highest point at 1,037 feet (316m), is a wildlife haven. There is also human history here, with the Iron Age hillfort on Wychbury Hill, and Clent Hill, where the 1st-century murder of St Kenelm took place. St Kenelm's Church is said to be built on the site of his demise – it is also the starting point for the 60-mile (97km) St Kenelm's Way and the location of one of the sources of the river Stour.

The Four Stones that stand at the top of Clent Hill have an ancient, pagan feel about them, particularly when the evening sun slants long shadows across the worn earth. In fact they were erected by Lord Lyttleton of nearby Hagley Hall in the 1750s, along with several other follies, including Wychbury Obelisk. It's a straightforward out-and-back walk to the stones from Nimmings car park – one which can be extended by following a circular route past St Kenelm's Church and over Walton Hill.

Challenge level: ✪✪✩✩✩
Start/finish: Nimmings Wood (NT) car park, Wood Lane, Hagley, B62 0NL
Distance: 3½ miles/6km
Map: OS Explorer 219

Local Highlights

→ Refuel at Nimmings Café, a local institution at Nimmings Wood car park.
→ Explore nearby Kinver Edge, with its heather-clad heathland and Iron Age hillfort. The rock houses here are also fascinating (paid entry/free for National Trust members).
→ The Clent Hills campsite (a Camping and Caravanning Club site but open to non-members) is brilliantly situated in a peaceful valley less than a mile (1.6km) from the hills.

Northern England

Home to some of Britain's most dramatic landscapes, there are superb outdoor adventures to be found here, from scrambling on knife-edge mountain ridges and swimming in cold, clear lakes to mountain biking on outstanding singletrack trails.

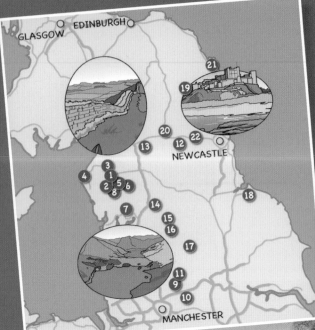

The Northern Lake District

The northern Lakes' high fells are a place of contrasts, with craggy mountain tops overlooking peaceful stretches of open water. Swimming is permitted in most of the lakes, though not in Ennerdale Water, Haweswater or Thirlmere.

The Southern Lake District

Home to England's highest mountain and largest lake, this region has a wealth of great adventure challenges to complete, as well as remote spots to explore at your own pace.

The North & South Pennines

Within easy reach of Manchester, Bradford and Huddersfield, the open moorland and rolling hills of the South Pennines provide a wonderful escape, with some wild-feeling places to explore. There is also excellent cycling, fell running and rock climbing here and a particularly dense network of public footpaths.

The North Pennines boast wild heather moorland criss-crossed with trails perfect for mountain biking and running; deep dales and upland rivers, many with cascading falls and plunge pools for a wild swim. Several important historical trails run across the moors, including a section of the Pennine Way.

The Yorkshire Dales & the North York Moors

The Yorkshire Dales National Park showcases some of the UK's finest limestone scenery, and its meadows, waterfalls and ancient broadleaved woodland contrast with the scattered remains of its industrial past. The neighbouring North York Moors is England's largest area of heather moorland, a high, wild place cut through by deep, wooded dales.

Northumberland

England's most northerly county boasts Kielder Water, the largest man-made lake in northern Europe. The vast open expanses of the Cheviots invite exploration, while the long stretch of coast is dotted with castles, sandy beaches, seals and puffins. Hadrian's Wall, the world's largest Roman artefact, stretches right across the country.

Ride the Altura Trail

Whinlatter Forest, owned by the Forestry Commission, is England's only true mountain forest. Although the summit of Whinlatter itself is bare, the surrounding fells and slopes are densely forested, scored through with winding trails that overlook Derwentwater and Bassenthwaite Lake. The Forest Park is home to the longest purpose-built mountain bike trail in the Lake District, the Altura Trail. The trail is 12 miles (19km) in length, 9 (14) of which are singletrack, and it takes you to a height of 500 m. It is graded a red route, so you'll need a reasonable level of mountain biking skill to ride it, but for those happy to take on the challenge, there's a fantastic selection of berms, jumps, rock features, skinnies, corkscrews and table tops. There are also blue-graded trails, suitable for all, which include a new mountain bike orienteering

Challenge level: ✪✪✪✪✪ **(Altura Trail)**
Location: Whinlatter Forest Park, CA12 5TW
Distance: 12 miles/19km
Map: OS Explorer OL4

route – great for teaching younger adventurers the art of map and compass navigation.

There's also bike hire, a café and lots of walking and running trails to explore, and during the summer months you can watch the Bassenthwaite ospreys soaring over Dodd Wood.

Local Highlights

➝ Camp at Lane Foot Farm, right at the foot of Whinlatter, where you'll find great facilities, glorious views and a warm welcome, particularly if you're a cyclist (stayinthornthwaite.co.uk)..

➝ Refuel at the Hungry Heifer Café at Keswick Climbing Wall – also a perfect spot for a rainy-day adventure.

2 Swimrun Buttermere ⚉ ⚙

The Lake District is a swimrunner's paradise, with countless lakes and tarns scattered across the trail-strewn fells.

Breca Swimrun's Buttermere event is a fantastic celebration of both the growing sport of swimrun and the Lake District, with its high, imposing fells scored with inviting trails, its clean, clear water for swimming, and its rocky platforms for jumping and diving. The sight of several hundred athletes powering through the water and scrambling the craggy hilltops is incredible. The swimming is divided between Buttermere and Crummock Water, but if you come here intending to have a quiet swimrun

adventure of your own, a circumnavigation of Crummock Water is a ready-made course, with long, lakeside run sections and swims across the 'coves'. There is one particularly wonderful figure-of-eight crossing of the lake, where rocky spits reach out into the water between Hause Point and Low Ling Crag. Sourmilk Ghyll, running from Blaeberry Tarn down to the northern tip of Buttermere, is an enjoyable scramble.

Challenge level: ✪✪✪✪☆
Start/finish: Buttermere car park, CA13 9UZ
Distance: 8 miles/13km (combined swim and run distance)
Map: OS Explorer OL4

Local Highlights

➡ Croft House Farm café, near to the car park, serves great food and has its own version of Butterbeer. There's free wifi and outdoor seating so you can make the most of the views.

➡ Wake up to the stunning Buttermere mountains at Skye Farm campsite – there's a tearoom and they even make their own ice cream. Tents only.

➡ Try the real Breca Buttermere swimrun event, held annually in August (www.brecaswimrun.com).

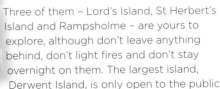

Local Highlights

→ Jump on a boat across to Hawes End or Low Brandelhow and walk up Catbells, one of the Lake District's friendliest high fells.
→ Visit the Keswick Mountain Festival, with music, inspiring talks, workshops and great food and drink, held annually on the shores of Derwentwater.
→ Stay with local adventurers Ruth and James at Cumbria House in Keswick (www.cumbriahouse.co.uk).

Derwentwater, nestled in the beautiful Borrowdale Valley, offers great opportunities for a paddling adventure, whether you're spending the day exploring the lesser-visited reaches in a kayak or stand-up-paddleboarding around the islands. You can launch from the Foreshore, Lodore, Nichol End or Portinscale, and you'll find gently shelving shores, islands for landing and exploration, plenty of hire centres and some wonderfully dramatic surroundings. There's a 10-mile (16km) lakeshore trail, which makes a great run, and direct access into the surrounding mountains for grander adventures. Look out for red squirrels and common sandpipers; this is also home to a healthy population of Britain's rarest fish, the vendace.

Derwentwater's four islands are all owned by the National Trust.

Three of them – Lord's Island, St Herbert's Island and Rampsholme – are yours to explore, although don't leave anything behind, don't light fires and don't stay overnight on them. The largest island, Derwent Island, is only open to the public on certain days each year, so please don't land here. The Foreshore is only a five-minute walk from Keswick town centre, and there's a National Trust shop and information centre. Boat hire is available at Derwentwater Marina (derwentwatermarina.co.uk), as is a range of self-catering accommodation.

Challenge level: ✪✪✩✩✩
Location: Derwentwater Foreshore, Keswick, CA12 5DJ
Map: OS Explorer OL4

4 Ride the C2C

Although not all of it is within the bounds of the Lake District National Park, this classic challenge rides right across it. The C2C was developed by Sustrans and partners and opened in 1994. Often considered to be the UK's most popular Challenge' cycle route, it

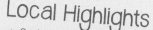

Local Highlights

→ Saddle Skedaddle offers fully-supported cycling holidays on the C2C and further afield (www.skedaddle.co.uk).

→ Keep an eye out for specially commissioned works by local artists along the route, including Sally Matthews's four steel cows at Consett and Tony Cragg's *Terris Novalis*, an epic steel sculpture of a theodolite which stands 6 metres high alongside the trail.

goes from the Irish Sea to the North Sea, from Cumbria to Tyneside. Both road and mountain bikes are suitable for the C2C – about half of it is off-road, and there are some rougher sections along the route, but there's always a surfaced alternative. There are also several route variations along the way, so you can choose to spend a few days leisurely riding the scenic longer route, or go for a single-day attempt on the shortest.

Starting in Whitehaven or Workington, and finishing in Sunderland, Wearside or Tynemouth, the route passes through the northern Lake District, Penrith and the Eden Valley before climbing the Pennines. Winding through old mining towns, it descends to the railway paths of County Durham. It includes Black Hill, the highest point on the National Cycle Network at 609 m, and the Consett & Sunderland railway path and sculpture trail.

The route is best ridden from west to east to take advantage of the prevailing winds and kinder gradients – longer downhill sections and shorter uphills. Keep with tradition and dip your back wheel in the Irish Sea at the start and your front wheel in the North Sea at the finish.

The route: National Route 71 between Whitehaven and Penrith; then National Route 7 between Penrith, Consett and Sunderland, or National Route 14 between Consett and Tynemouth: www.c2c-guide.co.uk. The following websites are packed with information on riding the C2C: www.sustrans.org.uk/route/sea-sea-c2c and www.c2c-guide.co.uk.

Challenge level: ✪✪✪✪✩
Start: Whitehaven railway station, CA28 6AX
Finish: Tynemouth, NE30 4RE
Distance: 140 miles/225km
Maps: OS Explorer OL4, OL5, OL31, 303, 307 and 316

5 Swim Grasmere to Rydal Water

the river and then swim the length of Rydal Water to reach Rydal village – a total of about 2 miles (3.2km) of swimming, depending on your route. On a warm day, or if you stow some clothes in a drybag, it's a lovely run back around the southern edge of the lakes to Grasmere.

Local Highlights

→ Walk through Rydal village, passing Rydal Mount, former home of William Wordsworth, to find the waterfalls and inviting pools at Rydal Bower.
→ Camp either at YHA Grasmere, an ideal spot from which to explore the surrounding fells and Sourmilk Ghyll, or at Tarn Foot Farm on the edge of Loughrigg Tarn.
→ Grasmere has a great selection of cafés and ice-cream sellers, enabling you to refuel after your adventure, as well as a couple of good outdoor shops.
→ Swim the Lakes, based in Ambleside, offers guided swims, courses, holidays and a well-stocked shop (www.swimthelakes.co.uk).

Grasmere and Rydal Water are both excellent lakes for swimming, with fewer boats than some of the busier lakes. Rydal in particular is peaceful, relatively warm and easy to access. The two lakes are joined by a stream, which makes for a wonderful adventure swim. The easiest way is to enter Grasmere at the beach in the south-eastern corner, just below Loughrigg Terrace. The entrance to the river is just here; follow this downstream to reach Rydal Water. The varying temperatures and textures of the water are incredible to experience as you swim. If you fancy a longer adventure you can start in Grasmere village and swim right across the lake to the mouth of the river, head down

Challenge level: ★★☆☆☆
Start/finish: access at south-eastern corner of Grasmere
OS grid ref: NY 342059
Distance: 2 miles/3.2km
Map: OS Explorer OL7

6 Scramble Long Crag

Long Crag is an awe-inspiring, sheer rocky buttress that rises up from just above the village of Coniston at the entrance to the Coppermines Valley. It's a classic Grade I scramble – the rock is grippy and the moves are engaging; however it is also a steep crag in a very elevated and exposed position, so you'll need a good head for heights. Good walking boots or fell shoes are fine for the ascent, but sticky rubber-soled rock shoes would make it even more enjoyable (though you'll still need walking boots for the walk-in/out), and we'd advise against attempting it in wet or winter conditions unless you have the specific skills and equipment to do so. There's no single correct line up the crag, so if you find you are wandering into tricky territory at any point, traverse until you reach easier ground. You'll find there's a great choice of lines up the rock, with something to entertain every level of scrambler. The finish of the

Local Highlights
➡ Camp at the National Trust's Hoathwaite campsite, right on the shores of Coniston Water, LA21 8AX. Launch your own boat from the campsite, or hire one from the Coniston Boating Centre, a not-for-profit organisation owned by the Lake District National Park, with all profits going to local conservation (www.conistonboatingcentre.co.uk).
➡ Sample a local ale at the Sun Inn, Coniston, Donald Campbell's HQ during his final attempt at the world water speed record.

Challenge level: ✪✪✪✪✫
Start/finish: entrance to Coppermines Valley, Coniston
OS grid ref: SD 299979
Distance: ¾ mile/1km from Coniston centre to top of Long Crag
Map: OS Explorer OL6

scramble leaves you part-way up Wetherlam; from here you have a choice: you can head left into the valley and follow the path back down to the start, link in with other scrambles in the Coppermines Valley, or head out over the fell tops. A particularly good route traverses the Prison Band across to the Old Man of Coniston.

7 Paddle Windermere

Windermere has a bit of a reputation for being busy, and thanks to its accessibility it is, in places. But don't let this put you off; venture to the lake's quieter shores and it's as peaceful a place as you could wish to find. At 11 miles long by a mile across, Windermere is the largest natural lake in England, its ribbon shape a glacial trough, formed some 13,000 years ago. It's deep too – up to 66 m in places – and a rich wildlife habitat, with large populations of fish, waterbirds and migrating geese in the winter. The paddle begins at Fell Foot, a brilliant place for adventures in its own right. Owned by the National Trust, it has something for everyone, from activities and watersports for families to a weekly parkrun. Regular buses run from Windermere railway station to Fell Foot.

As well as offering the excellent Challenge of completing an 11-mile (17.7km) paddle on its waters, Windermere also earns its place in this book through being one of the lakes included in British Canoeing's Three Lakes Challenge. The other two are Llyn Tegid (Bala Lake) in Wales (7 miles/11km) and Loch Awe in Scotland (25 miles/40km), the aim being to paddle all three. We're not keen on recommending adventures with elements located in different areas, requiring large amounts of driving to get between them; in this case, however, each lake is located in a place with much adventure potential,

so how about spreading the challenge over three separate trips, exploring each area while you're there?

Challenge level: ★★★★☆
Start: Fell Foot Newby Bridge, Windermere, Cumbria, LA12 8NN
OS grid ref: SD 380867
Finish: Waterhead
OS grid ref: NY 376032
Distance 11 miles/17.7km
Map: OS Explorer OL7

Local Highlights

➡ Ride the North Face mountain bike trail, a 10-mile/16km red-graded route in Grizedale Forest.

➡ Camp – or glamp – at the National Trust Low Wray campsite, right on the peaceful western shores of Windermere. Kayak hire is available here.

➡ Refuel with ethically sourced food and beers brewed on-site at the Drunken Duck, Barngates, LA22 0NG.

8 The Langdale Pikes

> No mountain profile arrests and excites the attention more than that of the Langdale Pikes and no mountain group better illustrates the dramatic appeal of a sudden rising of the vertical from the horizontal.
>
> *Alfred Wainwright*

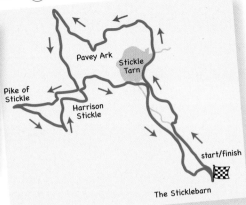

The Sticklebarn

Basing ourselves at the National Trust campsite right in the heart of the mountains, we've had the pleasure of spending many weeks exploring the Great Langdale valley, and yet every time we arrive after a period of absence we're amazed by the view. Following the winding road alongside the wide, flat, grassy valley floor, the sudden appearance of the combined jagged, vertical towers of the Pikes against the dark backdrop of Bowfell and Crinkle Crags is just awe-inspiring.

turn right and skirt the tarn, bearing right at its north-east corner and following the path due north to ascend the eastern flank of Pavey Ark. From the summit, head WNW to Thunacar Knott and then SW across Harrison Combe to Pike of Stickle. Descend Pike of Stickle by the same path and then ascend Loft Crag. From the summit, head NE to Harrison Stickle, taking in the summit of Thorn Crag and the head of Dungeon Ghyll as you go. From Harrison Stickle descend to the southern shore of Stickle Tarn before returning back down Stickle Ghyll to the start.

Challenge level: ✪✪✪✪✪
Start/finish: National Trust Sticklebarn car park, LA22 9JU
OS grid ref: NY294063
Distance: 5½ miles/9km
Map: OS Explorer OL6

The Langdale Pikes loop is a classic walk, and rightly so. The navigation is straightforward in good visibility and the walking isn't overly technical, but takes you to some airy peaks with magnificent views of the surrounding fells. The following directions are merely a guide; plan your route on the relevant map and take it – and good navigation skills – with you. This route is particularly tricky to navigate in poor visibility and shouldn't be attempted in winter conditions without specialist equipment and skills.

The route: from the National Trust car park, follow the path up to the left and behind the Sticklebarn pub, continuing to follow it straight ahead as it ascends steeply alongside Stickle Ghyll. Reaching Stickle Tarn at the top,

Local Highlights

➡ Look out for juniper trees – one of only three species of conifer native to Britain – which flourish here. The National Trust is currently running a juniper planting programme.
➡ The Sticklebarn pub leads a weekly guided running group, very helpful if you're looking for some great trails in the area.
➡ Relax with a real ale at the Old Dungeon Ghyll pub, a classic favourite with walkers and climbers.

9 Swim at Gaddings Dam

Local Highlights

➡ Climb to the 1,312-foot (400m) summit of Stoodley Pike, topped with the 121-foot-high (37m) Stoodley Pike Monument, built in 1856 after its predecessor was destroyed by lightning. You can climb the 39 steps to the top for fine views out over the surrounding moorland (access is free).

➡ Stay at Height Gate Farm, a 17th-century former farmhouse that sleeps groups of up to 30 in self-catering accommodation (www.heightgate.org.uk).

➡ Refuel at the Stubbing Wharf pub, right by the canal in pretty Hebden Bridge.

England's highest beach is at Gaddings Dam, an earth embankment dam located on top of the moors between Todmorden and Walsden. Constructed in 1833 to supply water to the mills of Lumbutts, the reservoir fell into disuse when the mills began to use steam power. It was rescued by a determined group of locals who bought the dam, repaired it, and now continue to maintain it (please consider supporting their efforts with an online donation at www.gaddingsdam.org). It's an incredible, wild place to swim, with vast skies stretching over the quiet water.

To add to the adventure, there is no road access to the dam – it's reachable only by a rough footpath across the moors. There's a station at Todmorden, and it's an excellent 45-minute walk or 20-minute run from here to the dam. If you're running we'd advise taking in a longer loop, exploring the fantastic trails around the area before finishing with a refreshing swim at Gaddings. Parking can be a real issue, particularly at busy times. On quieter days you may be able to park on Lumbutts Road, but on busier days this won't be possible and there's strictly no parking at the Shepherd's Rest car park unless you're using the pub. Be aware that there's no lifeguard cover here and that the nearest road is some distance away.

Challenge level: ✪✪✩✩✩
Location: Gaddings Dam, OL14 6JJ (nearest postcode)
OS grid ref: SD 949224
Map: OS Explorer OL21

10 The Stanza Stones Trail

The Stanza Stones Trail runs for 47 miles (76km) across the wild South Pennine countryside from Marsden to Ilkley, passing through Hebden Bridge and Bingley along the way. It starts and finishes at railway stations, with several others en route, and there are a number of campsites along the way too, making it a perfect route for a long weekend in the hills.

The trail is an inspiring tale of community, literature, art and a love for the great outdoors. In 2010 Ilkley Literature Festival commissioned well-known local poet Simon Armitage to create a series of poems responding to the landscape of the Pennine watershed, and letter-carver Pip Hall and her apprentice Wayne Hart to carve Simon's poems in six atmospheric locations along the watershed. At each end of the trail, on Pule Hill and Ilkley Moor, local drystone waller Nick Ferguson created a poetry seat where you can sit and admire the view or even write your own poem. The project also involved young people from local communities, some of whom had never been on the moors before. Armitage says of the project: 'as well as being landmarks in their own right, I hope the Stanza Stones act as beacons of inspiration, encouraging people to engage with West Yorkshire and Lancashire's great outdoors in thought, word and deed.'

Challenge level: ✪✪✪✪✰
Start: Marsden railway station, near Huddersfield, HD7 6AX
Finish: Ilkley railway station, LS29 8HF
Distance: 47 miles/76km
Maps: OS Explorer OL21, 288, 297

Local Highlights

→ Climb to the top of nearby Otley Chevin to take in the surprise views and enjoy the trails through the forest park.
→ Visit the Cow and Calf rocks, also known as Hangingstone Rocks, high on Ilkley Moor – and don't forget your hat.

|| Ride the Mary Towneley Loop

Local Highlights

→ Gisburn Forest has an outstanding mountain biking trail centre, with a route to suit everyone (www.gisburnbiketrails.com/).The Pennine Bridleway in its entirety is a great multi-day bikepacking challenge, running 205 miles (330km) between Cumbria and Derbyshire and specifically designed to be explored by horse or mountain bike.

The South Pennines is well known for its great-quality cycling, and there's an annual Walk and Ride Festival each September. The area boasts the country's longest continuous uphill road climb out of Cragg Vale towards Littleborough – definitely one to try when you visit.

The Mary Towneley Loop, named after Lady Mary Towneley, a strong supporter of public access to the Pennines, is a 47-mile (76km) bridleway loop through Rossendale, Calderdale and Rochdale that takes in part of the Pennine Bridleway National Trail. It's well waymarked and takes in a variety of surfaces, including grass tracks, stone setts

and causeways, aggregate paths and some quiet roads. Throughout the loop there are user-friendly gates, as well as pegasus crossings at main roads and clear signposting. The route is hilly and steep in places and takes you out into some remote places where shops are few and far between, so it's a great challenge in self-reliance too. Hebden Bridge, with its shops, cafés, accommodation and railway station, is a great place to start and finish the ride, but you can of course access it from any point on the circuit. There's an organised Mary Towneley Loop challenge each September, raising money for the Rossendale and Pendle Mountain Rescue Team.

Challenge level: ✪✪✪✪✪
Start/finish: A646 south-west of Hebden Bridge, OL14 6ED
OS grid ref: SD 969262
Distance: 47 miles/76km
Map: OS Explorer OL21

12 Isaac's Tea Trail

Once described as 'England's last great undiscovered wilderness trek', this challenging, waymarked 36-mile (58km) loop around the North Pennines takes in high moorland and river valleys, with over 4,900 feet (1,500m) of ascent. It begins in Allendale Town and visits the East Allen River, Carrshield Moor, Nenthead, River Nent, Alston, Blagill and the South Tyne River, returning over Ouston Fell. A great single- or two-day challenge at a run, it is traditionally walked over four days. The trail is named after local Victorian tea seller and philanthropist Isaac Holden, a familiar figure in his day walking the rough tracks over Allendale Common and Alston Moor. The route starts at Isaac's Well in Allendale and passes a number of Methodist chapels and other places associated with the Holden family. The moors and hay meadows are abuzz with wildlife – keep an eye out for lapwings, red squirrels and harebells as you go. Isaac's old hearse house near St Mark's Church in Ninebanks has been refurbished and now serves as a daytime walkers' shelter and information point for trail walkers.

Local Highlights

→ Watch the stars scattered across the vast Northumberland skies at Herding Hill Farm (herdinghillfarm.co.uk), where you can choose from bell tents, tipis, wigwams or lodges – or bring your own tent.

→ The Sill near Hexham is the UK's National Landscape Discovery Centre. It's packed with inspiration and education and you'll come away looking at the world around you differently. Café and accommodation on site (www.thesill.org.uk).

Challenge level: up to ✪✪✪✪✪ if done in one go
Start/finish: Isaac's Well, Allendale, Northumberland, NE47 9BJ
OS grid ref: NY 838558
Distance: 36 miles/60km
Maps: OS Explorer OL31 and OL43

/3 Geltsdale and the Gelt Boulder

Situated in a grassy meadow surrounded by trees, this lovely fine-grained quartzite boulder has something of an international reputation, having once been accidentally included in a guidebook on European climbing.

The Gelt Boulder can be found at the edge of the river Gelt about 7 miles (11km) south-east of Brampton. It's about 20 feet (6m) high with steep, sometimes slightly overhanging climbing and a perfect, cushioned, grassy landing. A short walk downstream brings you to an excellent swimming

pool below a waterfall in the clean water of the Gelt, where you can enjoy a post-climb dip or a day's playing with the family. The valley itself is magical and makes for a perfect day's exploring – or head up to Talkin Fell for spectacular views out across the Pennine landscape and a wander around the long line of cairns that adorns the summit.

Challenge level: varies
Location: east of Castle Carrock, CA8 9NF
OS grid ref: NY 557555
Map: OS Explorer 315

Local Highlights

→ Take a trip to the nearby village of Brampton, built from the local red sandstone and nestled in a glacial hollow. To the east of the village is a motte – the site of a medieval castle and beacon, now topped with a monument. The long, tree-lined ridge that stretches north-east from here is a wonderful walk or run.

→ Refuel at the excellent Blacksmiths Arms pub on the green in Talkin, just north of the Gelt Boulder.

14 Bike Bowderdale Beck ◉

The Howgills lie east of the Lakes and are a great place to head for a quieter day on the hills. The trails here very much follow the rolling undulations of the fells, alternating between tough uphill slogs and long, glorious downhill stretches.

The classic Howgills mountain bike route,

Local Highlights

➡ Visit Cautley Spout, England's highest above-ground waterfall. The broken cascade of falls tumbles nearly 650 feet (200m) down a series of rocky cliffs, starting from the high plateau of The Calf.
➡ Refuel at the Three Hares in the centre of Sedburgh.

graded a black route and therefore best for more experienced riders, starts with a long, tough climb from Sedbergh up to the Calf, which, at 2,218 feet (676m), is the summit of the Howgills. From here there's a fantastic long descent – 4 miles (6.4km) – down into Bowderdale. There are gates aplenty along the way, and expect some sections of pushing/carrying unless you're super-fit. This ride is made MUCH tougher by poor weather, in

particular high winds, and is at its best after a long, dry spell.

The route: from the centre of Sedbergh head north on Howgill Lane. At Lockbank Farm turn right onto the bridleway and follow this, bearing north, all the way to the Calf. From here enjoy 4 miles (6.4km) of singletrack into Bowderdale, following lanes through Bowderdale village. Just before the A685 turn right on tracks and minor roads through Weasdale to Ravenstonedale. Follow the lane south until it becomes a track at Adamthwaite, then continue south, joining and following the bridleway along the river Rawthey to return to Sedbergh.

Challenge level: ✪✪✪✪✪
Start/finish: Sedburgh, LA10 5AB
OS grid ref: SD 658921
Distance: 24 miles/38km
Map: OS Explorer OL19

15 The Yorkshire Three Peaks

Every year, on the last weekend in April, nearly a thousand runners line up at the start of the Three Peaks Race. Seven hundred or so finish, a combination of tough terrain and strict cut-off times seeing some off. The fastest finish in under three hours, though many take twice as long. The course, 24 miles (39km) long with 5,200 feet (1,585m) of ascent, is over the Yorkshire Three Peaks: Whernside (2,415 feet/736m), Ingleborough (2,372 feet/723m) and Pen-y-Ghent (2,277 feet/694m). These

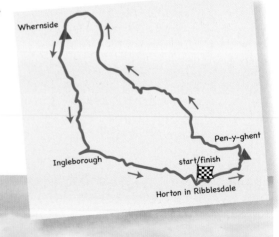

mountains form part of the Pennine range, encircling the heads of the valleys of Chapel-le-Dale and the river Ribble. The race has been held since 1954 and has gained a reputation as an absolute classic on the fell-racing calendar. There's also a Three Peaks Cyclo-Cross race that follows a longer 38-mile (61km) route across the peaks.

As well as being a must-do race for serious fell runners, the Yorkshire Three Peaks is a popular anytime challenge. Most people aim to complete the route in under 12 hours, starting and finishing in Horton-in-Ribblesdale.

The route: full details can be found at www.threepeakschallenge.uk and full planning with the relevant mapping is required. From Horton

Local Highlights

→ There's a wealth of discoveries to be made in the area, including Gaping Gill, England's highest waterfall; the remains of a huge Iron Age hillfort on the summit of Ingleborough; a fascinating network of caves, including the White Scar Caves; and vast areas of limestone pavement.

head south out of the village, then east to summit Pen-y-Ghent. Head generally north-east to Whernside, then south to Ingleborough, returning south-east to Horton.

Challenge level: ✪✪✪✪✪
Start/finish: Horton-in-Ribblesdale, **BD24 0HE**
OS grid rf: SD 808724
Distance: 24 miles/38km
Map: OS Explorer OL2

The Adventurer's Guide to Britain

16 Scramble Gordale Scar 🏛

> Let thy feet repair to Gordale chasm,
> terrific as the lair where the young
> lions couch.
>
> *William Wordsworth*

Gordale Scar is a limestone ravine north-east of the village of Malham where Gordale Beck flows down the craggy hillside. Two waterfalls tumble over the overhanging limestone cliffs from a height of over 328 feet (100m). On the right-hand side of the waterfalls is a classic Grade I scramble that follows limestone flakes and jugs up the scar, or if the water isn't flowing too strongly you can take your pick of the many different routes up the scar.

One of the best ways to experience Gordale and its intriguing surroundings is by going on a circular walk from Malham. The walk initially passes by the picturesque Janet's Foss, where a pretty waterfall tumbles into an inviting pool, before reaching Gordale Scar. Climb up Gordale Scar and head on to Malham Tarn (no swimming) before heading back down the stepped dry valley to reach the limestone pavement at the top of Malham

Local Highlights

➡ Camp at Gordale Scar campsite right by Malham Beck – it's a wonderful way to immerse yourself fully in the unique landscape (malhamdale.com/camping).
➡ Stock up on supplies or relax with a coffee at Town End Farm Shop & Café (townendfarmshop.co.uk).

Cove. From here, follow the steps leading down to the majestic scoop of Malham Cove itself – home to some of the hardest sport climbing routes in the country – before returning to Malham village.

Challenge level: ✪✪✪☆☆
Start/finish: National Park Centre car park, Malham village, BD23 4DG
Distance: 7½ miles/12km
Map: OS Explorer OL2

17 Swim the Wharfe at Bolton Abbey

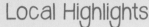

> On a bend in the river below the abbey ruins, there is a wide sandy beach and I fully expected to see John the Baptist rise up amongst the bathers and bless them all for having the sense and self-reliance to go swimming in the wild.
>
> Roger Deakin, WATERLOG

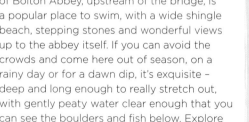

Its name deriving from the Old English woerf, meaning 'winding river', the river Wharfe flows 65 miles (105km) from Beckermonds, high in the central Yorkshire Dales, along the county boundary between North Yorkshire and West Yorkshire, and joins the river Ouse at Cawood, south of York. The stretch that curves gracefully past the ruins of Bolton Abbey, upstream of the bridge, is a popular place to swim, with a wide shingle beach, stepping stones and wonderful views up to the abbey itself. If you can avoid the crowds and come here out of season, on a rainy day or for a dawn dip, it's exquisite – deep and long enough to really stretch out, with gently peaty water clear enough that you can see the boulders and fish below. Explore

Local Highlights

➡ A little upstream, through ancient woodland, you'll come to the Strid – a narrow section of the river that has a fearsome reputation for swallowing people. Don't go in under any circumstances, but the walk alongside is delightful. Below the Strid there's some wonderful swimming in deep water through woodland.

➡ Stay at Catgill Campsite, less than a mile (1.6km) from the river, perfectly situated for exploring the area and for post-adventure refuelling at the Devonshire Arms and the Yorkshire Dales Ice Cream Factory. There's also Masons Campsite, just along the river, great for early-morning swims and with an onsite bakery and café.

➡ Read about the experience of author Joe Minihane (pictured) swimming here at jmtravels.org/floating.

upstream as below the bridge there's a weir. The water here is cold – wetsuit and footwear recommended.

Challenge level: ✪✪✩✩✩
Location: Bolton Abbey, near Skipton, North Yorkshire, BD23 6EX
OS grid ref: SE 076543
Map: OS Explorer OL2

18 Climb Roseberry Topping

Often described as Yorkshire's mini Matterhorn, the distinctive shape of Roseberry Topping makes it a popular and inviting challenge to climb. A sandstone outlier of the North York Moors uplands, until 1912 it was a sugarloaf (cone) shape; however, a geological fault, possibly in combination with local mining activity, caused it to collapse into its current shape. The hill was held in special regard by the Vikings, and Roseberry is a derivation of the name of the god Odin. This is a great place to run, as it also has the winding trails that run through the varied woodland and countryside at its foot – and it's always fun to reach a proper summit too. There's an annual Roseberry Topping Fell Race of 1.4 miles (2.3km) held each September by Esk Valley Fell Club.

The route: from the car park at Newton-under-Roseberry head south, skirting around Newton Wood and Cliff Ridge Wood. Then heading north again, climb over Roseberry Topping before turning left and contouring around the base of the hill to return to the start.

Challenge level: ★★☆☆☆
Start/finish: Newton-under-Roseberry car park, TS9 6QR
OS grid ref: NZ 570128
Distance: 5 miles/8km
Map: OS Explorer OL26

Local Highlights

→ Keep an eye out for fossils as you go – the rocks that form Roseberry Topping were laid down during the Jurassic period, and every step towards the summit represents around 5,000 years in geological time.
→ Enjoy cake and camping with fine Yorkshire views at Fletchers Farm in nearby Woodhouse (fletchers-farm.co.uk)

19 Across the Cheviots

The great granite plateau of the Cheviots was created by volcanic activity some 400 million years ago. Although it rises to a high point of 2,674 feet (815m) at the Cheviot summit itself, few of the hills are particularly prominent, creating a rising and falling ocean of open fell.

The final stage of the 267-mile (430km) Pennine Way crosses the Cheviots from Windy Gyle in the south right across the Cheviot Hills to Kirk Yetholm, just over the Scottish border, in the north. It's a wild and often bleak 27 miles (43km), with no civilisation along the way. It makes for an outstanding day's running, or a walk over two days, with a night on the hill or at one of the two B&Bs off the route, the latter adding a little extra to the total distance. There's also the option of making an excursion to the summit of the Cheviot, about a mile (1.6km) off the main path.

The route is waymarked throughout, though in poor visibility or when tired it is easy to miss a marker, so make sure you have a map, compass and navigational skills as it's a worrying place to get lost.

The annual Montane Spine Race tackles this stage at the end of a continuous traverse of the Pennine Way during winter conditions. The fastest runners will reach Kirk Yetholm in under 100 hours, but some may take over 160.

Challenge level: ✪✪✪✪✪
Start: Windy Gyle
OS grid ref: NT 855152
Finish: Kirk Yetholm, TD5 8PF
OS grid ref: NT 827281
Distance: 27 miles/43.5km
Map: OS Explorer OL16

Local Highlights

→ Tradition dictates that you should celebrate a successful Pennine Way adventure with a beer at the Border Hotel, just across into Scotland. This is also the start of the Scottish National Trail, which heads north for another 536 miles (862km) to Cape Wrath.

20 Hadrian's Wall & Broomlee Lough

With views of Hadrian's Wall rising and falling across the hills, Broomlee Lough is a beautifully positioned lake in a high moorland setting. It's a stone's throw from Housesteads Fort, and the Pennine Way runs right past it;

there are some fantastic running loops taking in the trails either side of Hadrian's Wall, and you can cool off in the lake afterwards. The approach is fairly marshy and parts of the lake are shallow; however, this does mean it warms up quickly, and the south-eastern corner, beneath Dove Crag, is deep enough for a good swim. This is one of the best-preserved sections of Hadrian's Wall and it's well worth walking up to it to appreciate the sheer scale of both the wall itself and the undertaking as a whole as it marches across the wild landscape, rising and falling with the steep, rolling hills. The Hadrian's Wall National Trail runs 84 miles (135km) from Wallsend in the east to Bowness in the west and makes a fantastic, and popular, adventure. Or you can cycle the 174-mile (280km) cycleway following NCN Route 72 across the country, some of it on the road and some of it traffic-free.

Challenge level: ✪✪✪✩✩
Location: Broomlee Lough, NE47 6NW
OS grid ref: NY 790697
Map: OS Explorer OL43

Local Highlights

➡ Sleep under the vast Northumberland skies at nearby Hadrian's Wall Camping and Caravan Site (www.hadrianswallcampsite.co.uk).
➡ Walk or run the 84-mile (135km) Hadrian's Wall Path – an incredible journey along the borders through millennia of human history.

The Farne Islands are a group of 15–20 (depending on the tide) islands, scattered in the North Sea between 1½ and 4½ miles (2.4 and 7.2km) off the Northumberland coast. Owned by the National Trust, they're a haven for wildlife, providing a nesting ground for over 100,000 seabirds, with 23 different species, including around 37,000 pairs of puffins. They're also home to a large grey seal colony, with more than 1,000 pups born every autumn.

For experienced sea kayakers and paddleboarders, the trip out to explore the islands is one of the best paddles in the country. You can launch from several locations, including Seahouses (there's a small fee) and Bamburgh. Avoid big tides and windy days, and be aware that there may be a bit of surf getting in. Local company Active 4 Seasons take guided sea kayaking trips out to the islands and many other locations around the area (www.active4seasons.co.uk). Or if you'd prefer to let someone else do the steering,

there are several boat trip companies that will take you out to the islands, departing from Seahouses. Landing is prohibited on most of the islands, and there are (friendly, helpful) National Trust rangers there frequently. You may be able to land on Longstone if conditions are right, but check before you go.

Challenge level: ✪✪✪✪✪
Location: Seahouses, NE68 7RN
OS grid ref: NU 219321
or Bamburgh, NE69 7AY
OS grid ref: NU 191345
Distance: 1½ miles/2.4km to reach the inner islands
Map: OS Explorer 340

Local Highlights

➡ Bamburgh Beach, with its long, sandy crescent and views up to the imposing Bamburgh Castle, is well worth a visit.
➡ The quirky Olde Ship Inn in Seahouses is good for a post-paddle pint.
➡ Just down the A1 you'll find Walkmill Campsite, friendly and unpretentious with pitches right by the river Coquet (walkmillcampsite.co.uk).

22 Ride Deadwater Fell, Kielder

Kielder Water and Forest Park is a haven for mountain biking, with several purpose-made trails. There's something for everyone, from the gentle rolling Green Trail through to the technical black-graded Deadwater Route. For an epic day's mountain biking, follow the Cross Border Trail, which links Kielder to the Scottish trail centre at Newcastleton, or tick off all the red trails in a single day. Our pick is the red-graded Deadwater Trail, which follows some great sections of technical singletrack and climbing, with a brilliant, flowy, bermed descent back to Kielder Castle. The optional black-graded loop to the top of Deadwater Fell is rewarded by an exciting descent if you fancy a longer and more challenging ride.

The wider Kielder Water and Forest Park area is well worth a few days' exploring. It's a dark sky reserve, perfect for stargazing, and the park is open 24 hours a day. There's a 26-mile (42km) lakeside way, great for running; in fact there's a Kielder marathon held on the route every year. You can stay on site should you wish, and you can even bring your own boat to go exploring on the lake, although you'll need to arrange insurance cover first. Entry to the park is free, though parking is £5 per day, which goes towards maintaining the park.

Challenge level: various
Location: Kielder Water and Forest Park,
NE48 1EP
OS grid ref: NY 631936
Map: OS Explorer OL42

Local Highlights

➡ Camp at Kielder Village Camping and Caravan Site, at the northern tip of Kielder Water and next to the remotest village in England – Kielder Village (kieldercampsite.co.uk).

➡ Make the most of some of the darkest skies in Europe and go stargazing down by the water.

➡ Have lunch by the stream at the family-run Pheasant Inn in nearby Stannersburn.

Wales

Making up just 9% of the UK's land mass, Wales has an incredible diversity of landscapes. Explore the spectacular coastline of Gower and Pembrokeshire; the sometimes rolling, sometimes rugged Brecon Beacons; and dramatic Snowdonia, where adventures are as challenging as you choose to make them.

Brecon Beacons

Stretching west from the English border the Brecon Beacons are a rolling, wild landscape. Their high point, Pen-y-Fan at 2,907 feet (886m), is also the highest point in South Wales. This area is a dark sky reserve, perfect for watching the stars.

Gower & Pembrokeshire

The rolling countryside of the Gower Peninsula is edged by a dramatic coastline and fantastic beaches, while Pembrokeshire boasts the UK's only coastal National Park. Here you'll find outstanding surf, great sea kayaking, exhilarating trail running and abundant wildlife, including seals and puffins.

Central & Eastern Wales

Mid-Wales's landscape is wild, rugged and sparsely populated and the hills rolling and often indistinct. It is the source of the Severn, the Wye and the Rheidol and is a place shrouded in ancient myth and legend.

The Berwyn Mountains lie relatively undiscovered between Snowdonia and the Wales/England border. Away from the crowds of the National Parks, this is a great place to explore if you're looking for real wilderness. The Offa's Dyke Path National Trail passes through eight different counties and crosses the border between England and Wales over 20 times.

Snowdonia

For many, Snowdonia is the ultimate adventure playground. Sparkling llŷns offer swimming of the wildest nature and there are jagged crags and outcrops famous for rock climbing. North Wales also has some absolutely brilliant scrambles, with lines such as Crib Goch on many an adventure ticklist.

Anglesey & the Llŷn Peninsula

Holy Island in Anglesey is the largest island in Wales and is dotted with the evidence of human habitation stretching over millennia. Most of the coastline is a designated AONB, and the Anglesey Coast Path is a great way to explore some of the most beautiful stretches of the island. The Llŷn Peninsula is a place of contrasts, from trendy Abersoch to peaceful farmland and stretches of wild, empty coastline.

Bikepack the Taff Trail

The Taff Trail is a mainly traffic-free 55-mile (89km) route that begins in Cardiff, taking in the sights of Wales's vibrant capital. It passes through towns rich in industrial and mining heritage before emerging into breathtaking mountain landscapes where waterfalls

cascade down craggy hillsides and twinkling reservoirs nestle in the valleys. The ride ends in the town of Brecon, a great place for a refuel or an overnight stop. From here you can either reverse the route to Cardiff or continue onwards, following the peaceful Monmouthshire and Brecon canal to the pretty town of Abergavenny, where there's a station and regular trains back to Cardiff. If you begin your ride in Brecon there's also

an outstanding loop that takes you all the way around Pen-y-Fan. Head out on the Taff Trail as far as Merthyr Tydfil before following bridleways and quiet lanes back north to Brecon.

Challenge level: ✪✪✪✪
Start: Cardiff Waterfront, CF10 5BZ
Finish: Market Street, Brecon, LD3 9DA
Distance: 55 miles/89km
Maps: OS Explorer OL12, OL13, 151 and 166

Local Highlights

➡ Stay at Pencelli Castle Caravan & Camping Park, just 4 miles (6.4km) from Brecon and right by the canal (www.pencelli-castle.com) or, for an amazing glamping experience, Aber Farm Shepherd's Hut in Talybont-on-Usk.
➡ Bike Park Wales in Merthyr is Britain's first full-scale mountain bike park and well worth a visit for anyone who enjoys getting out on the trails (paid entry).

2 Llanthony Priory Horseshoe

The part-ruined Augustinian priory at Llanthony, dating from around AD 1100, lies nestled in the steep-sided glaciated valley of the Vale of Ewyas. Entrance to the priory is free and it's a fascinating place to wander around; you can even picnic on the grassy surrounds. The surrounding Black Mountains, including the Hatterall Ridge, Hay Bluff, Twmpa, Rhos Dirion and Twyn Talycefn, create a wonderfully obvious challenge, yet one that's hard as nails, whether you're walking them in a day or running on them before lunch followed by a swim in the nearby river Honddu.

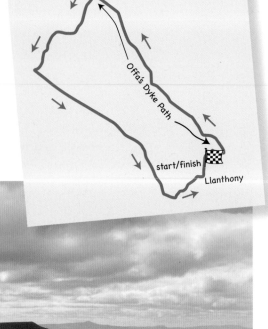

Local Highlights

→ Refuel in the Llanthony Priory Hotel, attached to the priory, which also has rooms in the 12th-century towers.
→ Camp in the shadows of the priory, with views out to the mountains at Llanthony Priory Campsite (www.llanthonycourt.co.uk).

The route: from the priory, head north, following signs to Hatterall Hill and Offa's Dyke Path. Climb steeply up to the top of the ridge and turn left, following Offa's Dyke Path along the top of the ridge for about 4 miles (6.4km). At Hay Bluff, marked by a trig point and the ending of the high ridge, turn left and descend, crossing the road at Gospel Pass and ascending steeply to the summit of Twmpa. From here, follow the ridge south-west to Rhos Dirion, turning left at the summit and following yet another glorious undulating ridge south-east, climbing over Twyn Talycefn and continuing until you reach the summit of Bal Mawr. Drop off the end of the ridge here, bearing left and descending steeply alongside Cwm Bwchel, eventually reaching the road at Llanthony.

Challenge level: ✪✪✪✪✪
Start/finish: Llanthony Priory, Llanthony, Abergavenny, NP7 7NN
Distance: 18 miles/30km
Map: OS Explorer OL13

3 Climb Pen-y-Fan

This is a popular and classic route in the Brecon Beacons, starting on Corn Du, the second-highest mountain in the Brecon Beacons at 2,864 feet (873m) and then taking in the soaring ridge across to Pen-y-Fan which, at 2,907 feet (886m), is the highest point in the Brecon Beacons and the highest point in South Wales.

The route: from the start, head west across the valley just before the reservoir and climb up to the obvious ridge. Head north along the ridge, bearing left at the path junction to reach summit of Corn Du. From here, head north-

west to the summit of Pen-y-Fan – the cairn on the summit is the remains of a Bronze Age burial chamber. Continue from Pen-y-Fan up a steep climb to Fan-y-Big for a breather and to take in the views. A clear track from Fan-y-Big takes you on a long descent – exhilarating if you're running the route back to the car park.

Local Highlights

➜ Wake up to views of the mountains at Pencelli Castle Campsite (www.pencelli-castle.com).

➜ Refuel at the National Park Visitor Centre – known locally as the Mountain Centre – on the north side of Pen-y-Fan in Libanus, Brecon.

Challenge level: ✪✪✪✪
Start/finish: Forest car park, 1½ miles/2.4km NW of Pentwyn Reservoir, CF48 2UT
OS grid ref: SO 032178
Distance: 8 miles/13km
Map: OS Explorer OL12

Waterfalls & Pools at Ystradfellte

At the southern end of the western Beacons lies Ystradfellte, a limestone landscape of lush wooded valleys in glorious contrast to the barren mountains of the north. Along 5 or so miles (8km) of the river valley are a series of beautiful waterfalls with clear, inviting pools. Along the river Nedd Fechan, Sgwd-y-Bedol (the Horseshoe Falls) cascades over several levels of semi-circular-shaped ledges, the sunlight making rainbows of the spray. A little further upstream, the water cascades over Sgwd Ddwli Isaf and Sgwd Ddwli Uchaf (the Lower and Upper Gushing Falls), below which lies a large open pool. On the Afon Hepste, an east-reaching branch of the Mellte, is Sgŵd yr Eira – Spout of Snow – where the footpath passes behind the waterfall.

A mile (1.6km) south of Ystradfellte the river Mellte disappears into the mouth of Porth-yr-Ogof (White Horse Cave), which has the largest cave entrance in Wales – it is nearly 66 feet (20m) wide and 10 feet (3m) high. The cave entrance is just a few minutes' walk from the car park; it is a steep climb down the worn and uneven limestone, but worth it to peer into the vast network of caves. If you want to explore further, specialist equipment is recommended and there are local caving guides who will show you the way.

Exploring the waterfalls, woods and caves and slipping into the various pools is a perfect way to spend a warm summer's day. To reach them, walk up the forest path from the Angel Inn at Pontneddfechan or park at Pont Melin-fach car park, off the Ystradfellte road, and walk downstream. Porth yr Ogof car park is nearest to White Horse Cave and manned most days – there is a car park charge of £3 per day.

Local Highlights

→ Nearby Clyngwyn Bunkhouse sleeps up to 19, ideal for a weekend away with friends.
→ Camp at Grawen Caravan & Camping Park, a few miles west of Ystradfellte (www.walescaravanandcamping.com).
→ Enjoy a local ale at the Angel Inn at Pontneddfechan.

Challenge level: ★☆☆☆☆
Location: Ystradfellte, Fforest Fawr, Powys, CF44 9JE
Map: OS Explorer OL13

5 swimrun Gower

The Gower and Swansea Bay Coast Path is part of the Wales Coast Path, an 870-mile (1,400km) long-distance route around the whole coast of Wales which opened in full in 2012. Starting in Rhossili village and heading east, the undulating, well-waymarked trail makes for some outstanding running, interesting underfoot yet brilliantly runnable without many of the leg-sappingly steep climbs you find on other stretches of coast – and the bays are just made for swimming across. Do not swim out to Worm's Head as there are strong currents here; however, the sheltered sections across Fall Bay, Port Eynon Bay, Oxwich Bay, Caswell Bay, Langland Bay and Bracelet Bay can be swum close to the shore in relative safety. If you're after an epic organised challenge, the Breca Swimrun Gower event held along this section of coast takes in all these and more, with 40km of running, 6km of swimming and 18 transitions, all with checkpoints and safety cover (www.brecaswimrun.com).

Local Highlights

➡ Refuel in the Bay Bistro in Rhossili village or the Beach hut Café at Mumbles Pier.
➡ Take a walk along Rhossili Down to the Beacon and then down to the 3-mile-wide (4.8km) sandy sweep of the bay. At low tide the oak ribs of the Helvetia, a Norwegian ship wrecked here in 1887, are visible, rising from the sand.

Challenge level: ✪✪✪✪✪
Start: Rhossili village, SA3 1PP
Finish: Mumbles Pier, SA3 4EN
Distance: full distance 28 miles/46km
Map: OS Explorer 164

6 Mountain Bike Gower

The classic Gower mountain bike route has a bit of everything, taking in the very best riding to be found here. It begins with a glorious stretch of ridge riding along the Gower Way, a 35-mile (56km) waymarked route that takes in some of the area's most important historical sites, followed by the only really technical singletrack on the loop (tricky in the wet). There's some outstanding riding alongside

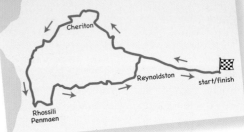

Challenge level: ✪✪✪✩✩ (blue grade with short red section)
Start/finish: Penmaen
OS grid ref: SS 530887
Distance: 19 miles/33km
Map: OS Explorer 164

beautiful Rhossili Bay, with glorious views out across the sea towards Worms Head, before heading enjoyably back to the start. There are a few stretches of road, and these can get busy during peak times over the summer, but the off-road trails are fantastic.

The route: from Penmaen follow the Gower Way to OS grid ref: SS 484 903, then Stembridge – Cheriton – Llangennith – Wales Coast Path to Rhossili – Gower Way back to Reynoldston and return to Penmaen.

Local Highlights

➝ Visit Penmaen Burrows and take in thousands of years of history; there's a Neolithic burial chamber, a Norman ringwork and a medieval church. Nearby Three Cliffs Bay, with its imposing limestone fins, is a beautiful beach to explore and very popular with rock climbers, boasting a range of easier-grade routes.
➝ Camp at Three Cliffs Bay campsite, waking up to stunning views out across the bay (threecliffsbay.com).

7 Run the Treginnis Peninsula

This route takes you around the Treginnis Peninsula, the extreme south-west point of the larger St David's Peninsula. It is formed from some of Wales's oldest rocks, the result of volcanic eruptions some 600 million years ago. This is a place that is equally joyous at all times of year, whether the summer flowers are in bloom or winter winds are chasing white-topped waves into St Brides Bay. Stop and catch your breath near the ruined 19th-century copper mine for fine views out to Skomer Island and the chance to spot porpoises in the ocean below.

Local Highlights

→ Stay at Porthclais Farm campsite, right on the Wales Coast Path with spectacular sea views (porthclais-farm-campsite.co.uk).
→ Make an evening of it at the award-winning Cwtch* restaurant in St David's.

The route: from Porthclais car park, take the quiet road right heading inland, turning left at the crossroads. At the road's end, follow tracks and paths north past the great rocky outcrop of Carn Trefeiddan before heading seaward on the road to St Justinian's. Here, join the coast path south, with truly spectacular views out to Ramsey Island. There is excellent running along the coast path here, with technical ascents and descents to keep it interesting. The final section winds through fine coastal heathland and down to the rocky and secluded cove of Porthlysgi. Continue on the coast path to Porthclais Harbour and back to the car park.

Challenge level: ⭐⭐⭐⭐⭐
Start/finish: Porthclais Harbour (NT) car park, SA62 6RR
OS grid ref: SM 739242
Distance: 6½ miles/10km
Map: OS Explorer OL35

8 Ride the Celtic Trail

The Celtic Trail spans the breadth of Wales, from Fishguard in the West to Chepstow on the English border. The western loop is a 144-mile (232km) tour of Pembrokeshire, with a short section in Carmarthenshire, using National Cycle Network Routes 4 and 47. Waymarked throughout, this is a sizeable challenge and an awesome adventure that really explores this beautiful corner of Wales. The brilliantly varied riding is on quiet roads, coastal trails, ancient trackways and riverside paths.

to Crymych in the Preseli Hills. From here the route heads through the National Park, over the hills dotted with standing stones – the ones used to build Stonehenge in Wiltshire. A final downhill stretch returns you to Fishguard. Depending on your preference, you could try the full route in a oner or break it down into 5–6 sections to give you a great week's holiday with plenty of time to explore.

The route: you can, of course, join the loop at any point that suits, though Fishguard makes a good starting point with its mainline station. From here the route heads south-west on NCN Route 4, following the Pembrokeshire coast through St David's and along St Brides Bay and the surfing hotspot of Newgale Beach. There are great views from here out to Ramsey Island and Skomer Island. From Broadhaven the ride heads off-road, following the Ridgeway, a Neolithic trackway, to Pembroke and Tenby. Quiet lanes wind past Laugharne Castle and the Boathouse, where Dylan Thomas wrote Under Milk Wood. Here the route joins the river Taf, following it upstream to St Clears and then Carmarthen. At Carmarthen we leave Route 4 and head back west on Route 47. Undulating lanes wind through river valleys and peaceful countryside

Challenge level: ✪✪✪✪✪

Start/finish: Fishguard seafront, SA64 0DE

OS grid ref: SM 946381

Distance: 144 miles/232km

Maps: OS Explorer OL35, OL36, 177 and 185

Local Highlights

➡ Visit Laugharne, home of Dylan Thomas, and take a stroll along the 'heron-priested shore', immersed in the views that inspired his writings.
➡ Jump on a boat over to Skomer Island to see the puffin colonies.

9 Bikepack the Trans-Cambrian Way

Local Highlights

→ Visit CAT, the Centre for Alternative Technology, just north of Machynllyth for a fascinating insight into eco-living and top tips on being green (www.cat.org.uk).
→ Go mountain biking in the Dyfi Valley. There are three waymarked routes (Mach 1, 2 and 3 along roads, lanes and bridleways) and Cli-MachX, an exhilarating off-road forest trail with rocky jumps and an epic final descent (www.dyfimountainbiking.org.uk).
→ Local guides Mountain Bike Wales offer expert guiding in Wales and beyond (www.mtb.wales).

Pioneered by members of the International Mountain Bike Association of the UK (IMBA), the Trans Cambrian Epic Ride is a 100-mile (161km) route from the English border to the Irish Sea across the remote hills and moorland of central Wales. The route has been designed to avoid main roads, gated field systems and farmyards, and largely uses moorland tracks and trails. Much of the riding is through remote and exposed areas, so it is essential to carry food, drink, maps, weatherproof clothing, tools, spares, first-aid kit – and an exit strategy, should you find yourself running out of daylight. There are some challenging descents and five major fords, all of which can be treacherous following heavy rain. Fortunately, all have optional bridges or are crossable upstream, so if in doubt, always take the safer option. There are many miles through farmland and it's essential that bikers respect the landowners and their property – please adhere to the Countryside Code, closing all gates securely behind you. Finally, please be aware of other users on the trail, in particular

on the final descent to the sea, as this is a popular route. A reasonably fit rider should be able to complete the challenge over three days, although day two is long and hilly, so make sure you leave early. Alternatively, you may prefer to ride it over a more relaxed four days. For those after a serious challenge, it can be done in a day, and the fastest time is currently around 12 hours. A comprehensive guide to the route is available free of charge from the IMBA website (imba.org.uk). Riding the Trans-Cambrian Way is epic indeed, but it's also a challenge that's rewarded with a huge sense of achievement.

Challenge level: ✪✪✪✪✪
Start: Knighton centre, LD7 1BL
OS grid ref: SO 286723
Finish: Dovey Junction, Machynlleth, SY20 8SU
OS grid ref: SH 744012
Distance: 100 miles/161km
Maps: OS Explorer 200, 201, 213 and 214

10 The Sarn Sabrina Challenge

Based on the Celtic myth of Sabrina, a water nymph said to inhabit the river Severn, the Sarn Sabrina Challenge is a 25-mile (40km) circular route that can be walked either as an anytime adventure or as part of the organised event which is held in May each year. Starting in Llanidloes, the route sets off along the Glyndwr's Way National Trail. Heading up past the Van Pool brings you to open hillside with extensive views of the Llyn Clywedog and the surrounding countryside, before following the shoreline of the lake to the borders of the Hafren Forest and Cwmbiga Farm. Climbing through the forest to the slopes of Plynlimon, the highest point in mid-Wales,

Local Highlights

➙ Glyndwr's Way itself is a fantastic longer adventure – 135 miles (217km) from Knighton to Welshpool via Machynllyth through many sites of Wales's cultural and natural history.
➙ Enjoy a local ale at the Crown and Anchor in Llanidloes, locally known as Ruby's after the landlady.
➙ Choose from a yurt, a shepherd's hut or a tipi at Cledan Valley Glamping (www.cledanvalley.co.uk).

countryside before arriving back in Llanidloes. Waymarked throughout with distinctive blue water nymphs, this is a tough challenge but hugely rewarding, whether you take part in the annual event or do it on your own. It makes a fantastic day's run too, with relatively straightforward navigation for this area. We'd advise taking a map and compass in case visibility is poor or you miss a waymarker. There's also the Semi-Sabrina, a 12-mile (19km) version of the route.

the trail then visits the source of the Severn at 2,034 feet (620m) above sea level. Descending through forest along the Severn Way long-distance path, the trail visits the watershed of the Severn and the Clywedog, enjoying stunning views of the surrounding

Challenge level: ✪✪✪✩✩
Start/finish: Llanidloes, Powys, SY18 6BN
Distance: 25 miles/40km
Map: OS Explorer 214

// The River Dee Canoe Trail

The northern stretch of the river Dee tumbles through Llangollen in a mass of turbulent white water, but lower down, once it has met its flood plain, the river becomes a gentle meander through scenic countryside. Although included in north-east Wales here, the majority of this adventure follows the border – for much of the trip you'll have Wales on one side and England on the other. The finish is right in the heart of Chester, a magnificent place to land.

Because of the nature of this stretch of the Dee there are no compulsory portages; however, the sole weir at Chester is avoidable if you prefer, via a portage on the left bank. To shoot the weir, stay left – but don't attempt to shoot it when the river is high. The put-in point is just upstream of the bridge at Farndon, where there's also a car park.

Challenge level: ★★★★☆
Start: Farndon Bridge, CH3 6QF, OS grid ref: SJ 412544
Finish: Queen's Park Suspension Bridge, Chester
OS grid ref: SJ 408659
Distance: 11 miles/18km
Maps: OS Explorer 257 and 266

Local Highlights

→ Make a weekend of it in September at the Goodlife Experience, a weekend of music, food, workshops, culture and tales of adventure on the Hawarden Estate.
→ Celebrate your successful descent at the excellent Old Harkers Arms, right by the canal.

12 Ride the Wayfarer

'Wayfarer' was the pen name of Walter MacGregor Robinson, a journalist and pioneer of off-road cycling. His writings in *Cycling* magazine inspired many others to get out exploring the trails and his popular lantern talks drew large crowds who would cycle long distances to hear him speak. After Wayfarer's death in 1956 a memorial was erected on the Bwlch Nant Rhyd Wilym, one of Wayfarer's favourite crossings.

There are three main route options to get you started. The first is a simple out-and-back ride up the pass to the memorial, a little over 5 miles (8km) each way. From Llanarmon head

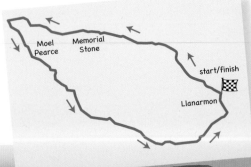

north-west up the lane, through Pentre, the landscape becoming more mountainous as you climb. Bear left where the road becomes a track and ascend alongside a stream trending north-west to reach the memorial at grid ref SJ 091365. Return the same way. For the second route, carry on at the memorial, heading west and bearing left at the fork. Continue along this track to reach the track junction at grid ref SJ 051375. For the 18-mile (29km) option, turn left here and follow the bridleway trending north over Moel Pearce and between the peaks of Cadair Berwyn and Cadair Bronwen. Staying on the bridleway, descend steeply to join the lane at grid ref SJ 098319. Work your way back along quiet lanes to return to Llanarmon. There is also a full, 30-mile (48km) classic loop: Llanarmon – Wayfarer pass – Llandrillo – Llangynog – Llanrhaeadr-ym-Mochnant – Llanarmon. Don't attempt either of the long routes in wet weather.

Challenge level: up to ✪✪✪✪✩
Start/finish: Llanarmon LL20 7LD
OS grid ref: SJ 156328
Distance: 10 miles/16km or 18 miles/30km or 30 miles/50km
Map: OS Explorer 255

Local Highlights

➥ Eat and stay at The Hand in Llanarmon, a favourite haunt of the Wayfarer himself (www.thehandhotel.co.uk).
➥ Camp at Dol-Llys Farm – picturesque Welsh countryside camping on the banks of the young River Severn, perfect for an early morning dip (dolllyscaravancampsite.co.uk).
➥ Riding with an experienced guide is a great way to get the most out of an area; we recommend Flattyres' knowledgeable, friendly guides (www.flattyres-mtb.co.uk).

13 Offa's Dyke & the Clwydian Range

The full length of the 177-mile (285km) Offa's Dyke Path National Trail makes a great adventure to walk over a week or two, following the regular acorn waymarkers and soaking up the varying and engaging landscapes. There are also many circular walks that use the trail. The final section of the Offa's Dyke Path runs through the Clwydian Hills, taking in the open upland vistas and chequered hillsides – an outstanding point-to-point adventure. Our route extends slightly past the official ends of the Clwydians, but in doing so it also starts and finishes conveniently at towns with railway stations,

with Iron Age hillforts and cloaked in heather and bilberry. The final stretch descends enjoyably off the ridge to greet the sea at Prestatyn.

Challenge level: ✪✪✪✪
Start: Chirk railway station, Chirk, Wrexham, LL14 5LT
Finish: Prestatyn railway station, Prestatyn, LL19 7ER
Distance 44 miles/71km
Maps: OS Explorer 201, 216, 240 and 256

making the logistics of the adventure fairly straightforward. The 44-mile (71km) journey from Chirk, just south of the hills, to the end of the trail at Prestatyn might take 2–3 days to walk or run, but the return part of the trip will have you back in just an hour. The route starts in Chirk, with its 14th-century castle and estate, owned by the National Trust. It crosses the Dee on the much-photographed Pontcysyllte Aqueduct and runs below the ancient fortress of Eglwyseg Rocks. A crossing of the bleak Llandegla Moor is a warm-up for the traverse of the Clwydian Range, dotted

Local Highlights

➡ Visit the Grade I listed, 13th-century Chirk Castle (National Trust) and walk around the stunning estate.
➡ Explore Llangollen, part of the UNESCO World Heritage Site that includes the 11 miles (18km) of canal from Gledrid to the Horseshoe Falls via the spectacular Pontcysyllte Aqueduct. There's a steam train or a horse-drawn boat available to discover the area if you're weary after your adventure.

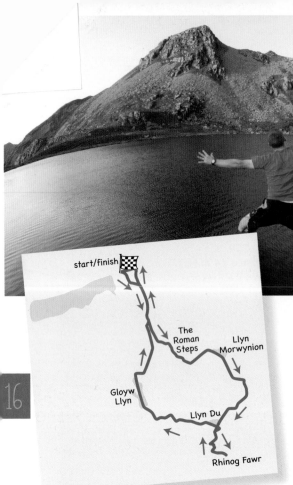

14 swim in the Rhinogydd

views before returning for a second swim of Llyn Du, this time heading west out through the notch and descending to the western shores of breathtaking Gloyw Llyn, the 'gleaming lake'. Swim the length of the lake before rejoining the path northwards to return to the car park.

Challenge level: ✪✪✪✪✪
Start/finish: Cwm Bychan car park 1¼ miles/2km NE of LL45 2PH
OS grid ref: SH 645314
Distance: 5 miles/8km
Map: OS Explorer OL18

The Rhinogydd mountains occupy a quiet, untamed corner of Snowdonia where rocky gullies and knife-edged peaks tower over forested river valleys. Exploring these mountains, it seems as though there's a llyn in every crevice, every long uphill slog rewarded by a glassy pool. Rhinog Fawr is one of the highest peaks in the range, rising to 2,362 feet (720m) at its summit. A perfect summer day's adventure can be found here, running, scrambling and swimming the llyns.

The route: from the start the route heads south on a footpath through woodland and then straight up the Roman Steps, the well-preserved remains of a medieval packhorse trail leading from Chester to Harlech Castle. If you're feeling brave you can drop down to the left and have a quick swim in Llyn Morwynion. At OS grid ref SH 66049 29906 turn right off the main path and ascend south and then south-west to Llyn Du for the next swim. From here an enjoyable scramble up a gully takes you to the summit of Rhinog Fawr. Enjoy the

Local Highlights

→ Stay at Dinas campsite in nearby Llanbedr, set in peaceful surroundings with campfires allowed (www.hideaway-in-the-hills.com).
→ Visit the vast, sandy beach at Harlech, backed by nature-rich dunes and the turreted medieval Harlech Castle.

15 Paddle Lake Bala

Lake Bala, also known as Llyn Tegid, lies in a glacial valley surrounded by mountain peaks. This is an area steeped in myth and legend, including one told by the 6th-century poet Taliesin about Tegid Foel and his wife, the witch Ceridwen, who lived by the lake. Another tells of the drowning of the old town of Bala by the evil prince Tegid Foel – the lake was named after the cruel prince and it is said that of a dark night the lights of the town can still be seen shining from the lake. Lake Bala is 3¾ miles (6km) long by 0.5

miles (0.8km) wide, and the out-and-back paddle is the Welsh stage of British Canoeing's Three Lakes Challenge, although if you're not concerned about the time you take, then a full circuit is a more interesting day out. The river Dee runs through the lake, meaning it is prone to sudden flooding, so don't attempt to paddle it during or after heavy rain. To paddle here, you'll need to purchase a permit from the Lake Warden's Office. Kayak and stand-up paddleboard hire is available from Bala Watersports on the foreshore, and whitewater rafting sessions are available at the National Whitewater Centre (from £35 pp).

Local Highlights

→ Stay at Bwch-yn-Uchaf Caravan and Camping Site, right at the edge of the lake (bwch-yn-uchaf.co.uk).
→ The Eagles Inn at Llanuwchllyn at the southern end of the lake serves locally sourced food and good beer.
→ Jump on the narrow-gauge Bala Lake Railway, run by volunteers, to see the area from a different perspective.

Challenge level: ✪✪✪✩✩
Start/finish: Lake Bala (Llyn Tegid) Foreshore, Bala, Gwynedd, LL23 7SR
Distance: 7 miles/11km out and back
Map: OS Explorer OL23

16 Scramble the North Face of Tryfan

Rising like a giant's backbone out of the Ogwen valley, Tryfan is one of Wales's most recognisable mountains, with many classic routes up to its 3,011-foot (917.5m) summit. Perhaps the most famous route up Tryfan is the North Ridge – a long and thrilling Grade I scramble that makes a perfect introduction to the activity. Looking up at the ridge from the A5 it rises skywards, compelling you to climb it. A great challenge for those finding their feet (and hands) in scrambling, the ridge has relatively straightforward terrain and low exposure. Don't underestimate the challenges though, particularly when it comes to navigation.

One of the biggest challenges is finding the right line to start with, particularly in poor visibility, so it's worth taking extra care when you begin to ensure you're heading up the right route, or you could find yourself on something much harder. Most scramblers start from the A5 lay-by directly below the North Ridge and follow the path to the left of Milestone Buttress. The path steepens and rises towards a large boulder field. Turn right here and scramble up loose scree to a steep step of rock. Climb up this and continue up the wide ridge, following some quartz slabs. Carry on straight up the North Tower for some the best views in the area. The final section finishes at the twin stones of Adam and Eve, and the traditional way to celebrate summiting Tryfan is to jump between these, if you dare. From here head down the South Ridge, either carrying on over Bristly Ridge for more wonderful scrambling or, for the shorter descent, turning right at Bwlch Tryfan and descending to the eastern shore of Llyn Bochlwyd and following the path north down Bochlwyd Buttress back to the main road.

NB: this route is relatively straightforward on a clear, dry day but a much more serious prospect in poor visibility, or in wet or winter conditions.

Challenge level: ✪✪✪✪✪
Start/finish: A5 lay-by just east of Idwal Cottage YHA
OS grid ref: SH 661602
Distance: 2½ miles/4km
Map: OS Explorer OL17

Local Highlights

→ There are two campsites at the foot of Tryfan: Gwern Gof Uchaf and Gwern Gof Isaf. Both are good and well positioned for exploring the area.

→ Tackle the incredible mountain ridges of the Glyderau, to the south of Tryfan, and the Carneddau, to the north.

→ Hire an experienced and knowledgeable guide from local adventure company Raw Adventures for the best Snowdonia experience (www.raw-adventures.co.uk).

17 cycle Snowdon

We were surprised – and excited – when we first discovered you're allowed to mountain bike to the top of Snowdon. It's well worth a trip, and it's an excellent alternative to the usual busy walk and summit crowds. The main reason for the lack of crowds on such trips is that there is a voluntary ban on riding here between 10am and 5pm from 1 May to 30 September, so two-wheeled expeditions on the mountain must be undertaken out of season or at dawn/dusk. Flattyres Mountain Biking offers guided excursions up the mountain (www.flattyres-mtb.co.uk).

The route: starting in Llanberis (SH 581599), head south towards Pen-y-Pass. At the mini roundabout turn right onto Victoria Terrace. Continue straight over the cattle grid, past the café and through a gate, taking the next left onto a bridleway signed 'Snowdon'. This is the Llanberis Path and it will take you all the way to the top – how much you ride and how much you push is up to you and your legs. On reaching the summit, admire the views and come back down the same way. If you're happy on more technical trails, you can also descend via the Snowdon Ranger Path, turning right at Maesgwm to return to Llanberis.

Challenge level: ✪✪✪✪✪
Start/finish: Llanberis
OS grid ref: SH 581599
Distance: 11 miles/18km
Map: OS Explorer OL17

Local Highlights

→ If you're confident in your mountain skills, the Snowdon Horseshoe is one of THE great challenges in North Wales. It curves around the eastern cwm of the massif in a great arc, linking the four principal summits. None of the scrambling is harder than Grade I, but it's sustained and the consequences of falling are often serious. The ridges of Crib Goch and Crib y Ddysgl, which leads to Snowdon's second highest peak Garnedd Ugain, are exposed and tricky to escape, but an incredible adventure. Don't attempt in poor weather.

18 Swim Llyn Padarn

Go exploring in the higher reaches of Snowdonia National Park and you'll find countless llyns and pools of a fantastic variety of shapes and sizes cradled within the features of the mountains. There's something utterly magical about reaching the top of a long, steep ascent on a hot summer's day and finding a deep, clear pool appearing like a mirage before you. This really is wild

Challenge level: ⭐⭐⭐⭐☆
Location: Llyn Padarn, Llanberis, LL55 4TY
Distance: 2 miles/3.2km end to end
Map: OS Explorer OL17

swimming at its absolute wildest and best.

Since 2014, Llyn Padarn on the edge of Llanberis village has been a designated freshwater bathing lake, its water quality carefully monitored under the Bathing Water Directive. The 2-mile (3.2km) stretch of outstanding open-water swimming is perfect for anyone looking for an endurance swim, and there are many lagoons and inlets to explore for a real adventure swim. This is also a great place to paddleboard – Snowdonia Watersports right on the lakeside offers guided paddles and tuition.

There is parking around the lake, and you can even catch the steam train that'll take you along the Llanberis Lake Railway to the start.

Local Highlights

→ Refuel at legendary climbers' cafe Pete's Eats in Llanberis, 'possibly the best caff in the world' (www.petes-eats.co.uk).
→ Camp at Camping in Llanberis (www.campinginllanberis.com), perfectly positioned for exploring Llyn Padarn and Snowdon.
→ Take part in the annual Love Swimrun Llanberis event held at the lake each June (www.loveswimrun.co.uk).

19 The Nantlle Ridge

Local Highlights

→ The Rhyd Ddu path up Snowdon also begins at the car park. A relatively secret way up the popular mountain, connoisseurs say it's the most peaceful and most beautiful way to the top. The final traverse of the Bwlch Main ridge is utter joy.

→ Local company Raw Adventures offers excursions with experienced and knowledgeable guides across Snowdonia (www.raw-adventures.co.uk).

Hidden in a peaceful corner of the north-west edge of Snowdonia, a few miles west of Snowdon itself, lies the Nantlle Valley. This is a place entrenched in history and legend that feels different and removed from the tourist-lined slopes nearby. The Nantlle Ridge is a grassy stride along elegant curved arêtes, linking all the summits in the range. The views are incredible, and worth picking a clear day for, and although there are plenty of sections with enough scrambling to make it more interesting than a straightforward ridge run, there's nothing that could be considered scary. There are some broad, grassy sections of the ridge that are up there with the best running experiences to be found on earth.

The route: start from Rhyd Ddu, using either the tiny station served by the narrow-gauge Welsh Highland Railway, which runs between Caernarfon and Porthmadog, or the National Park car park. Head west through the ornate gate on the other side of the road and follow the slate path towards the ridge. The traverse begins steeply with an ascent of Y Garn, at 2,077 feet (633m). Continuing along the rising and falling trail brings you to Mynydd Tal-y-Mignedd, topped with an obelisk built for Queen Victoria's Diamond Jubilee in 1897. The next summit is the high point of the ridge, Craig Cwm Silyn, at 2,408 feet (734m), from where the summits decrease in height again and the ridge finishes with Mynydd Graig Goch, at 610 m.

There are various options to turn the route into a loop, though you'll probably find, as we did, that on reaching the end you just want to turn around and do it all again. Llyn y Gader at the finish in Rhyd Ddu is a great place to cool off after a few hours' mountain running.

Challenge level: ✪✪✪✪
Start/finish: Rhyd Ddu Car Park, LL54 6TN
OS grid ref: SH 571527
Distance: 12 miles/19km out and back
(6 miles/9.5km each way)
Map: OS Explorer OL17

Wales : Snowdonia

20 Ride the Copper Trail ⚫

Anglesey was once one of the world's largest producers of copper, an industry going back thousands of years. The Copper Trail was designed to enable people to visit some of the fascinating sites of this important heritage that remain visible today. The route travels past Cemlyn Nature Reserve with its large lagoon, separated from the sea by a spectacular, naturally created shingle ridge. The reserve is home to many species of birds, wildflowers and marine creatures. It also passes Swtan – the island's last-remaining thatched cottage – Amlwch Port and the Copper Kingdom at Parys Mountain.

Local Highlights

→ Base yourself at the excellent Plas Lligwy Cottages, set in 300 acres of farmland and 90 acres of woodland which guests are free to explore. Within the farm's boundaries lie Din Lligwy, a Romano-British settlement dating from the 4th century, Hen Capel Lligwy, a tiny ruined 12th-century chapel and Lligwy Burial Chamber, a neolithic cromlech. It's only a short walk to Lligwy Beach, where you'll find a beach café (www.lligwy.co.uk).

Following a well-waymarked network of quiet lanes and paths along National Cycle Network Route 566, the Copper Trail explores the beautiful Anglesey coast between Llanddeusant in the west and Llanerchymedd in the east. Using a short section of NCN Route 5, it can be linked up to make an enjoyable 34-mile (55km) loop around the north of the island, with some gentle climbs but nothing too strenuous. There are two unsigned shortcut routes across the middle of the loop should you wish to shorten it. For a bigger adventure, you can ride the full loop around Anglesey, keeping to the coast – a ride of around 60 miles (97km) by the shortest route along primarily main roads, though this could be extended to use quieter routes

and explore further. The Copper Trail can be started at any point on the loop; it passes through the village of Llanfechell, where there is a pub and car park.

Challenge level: ✪✪✩✩✩
Start/finish: Llanfechell, Anglesey
OS grid ref: SH 369 912
Distance: 34 miles/55km
Maps: OS Explorer 262 and 263

21 Explore Holyhead Mountain

Local Highlights

➡ Refuel at the Black Lion in Holyhead, great for local food and ales (blacklionanglesey. com).

➡ Visit the Skerries, a small group of uninhabited islands just off Holyhead, home to a vast number of seabirds and an RSPB reserve. Regular boats from Holyhead.

At 722 feet (220m), Holyhead Mountain (Welsh: Mynydd Tŵr, from (pen)twr, meaning tower) is the highest hill in Anglesey, rising from the far north-west corner of the island and sloping steeply down to the Irish Sea on two sides. The summit views on a clear day stretch far across the sea to Ireland's Wicklow Mountains.

Being just a pint-sized mountain, it's easy to explore within the distance of just a few miles. One of our favourite routes makes for an enjoyable walk or run, although give yourself plenty of time to stop and take in the many interesting sights you pass along the way.

The route: from the Country Park head north-west directly onto the Coast Path and past the North Stack fog signal station, from where there are wonderful coastal views across to the rugged cliffs of South Stack. The path then winds its way southwards before climbing to the rocky, heather-clad summit with its fantastic views and Iron Age hill fort. Descending back to the Coast Path, the route goes through the South Stack part of the Seabird Centre, where you might spot puffins and oystercatchers. The final stretch takes you around the base of Holyhead Mountain and back to the Country Park.

Challenge level: ✪✪✪✪✪
Start/finish: Breakwater Country Park, Holyhead, LL65 1YG
OS grid ref: SH 225832
Distance: 5 miles/8km
Map: OS Explorer 262

123

22 Around Llanddwyn Island

Llanddwyn Island, or Ynys Llanddwyn, is not, in fact, quite an island, except at the very highest of tides. But, positioned at the mouth of the Menai Strait in the far south-west of Anglesey, it does feel removed and special, and completely different from the mainland – an island identity perhaps. Peaceful and serene in sunny weather, yet untamed and exhilarating in a storm, it's a perfect place to spend a few hours exploring, and a full circumnavigation is only an hour or two's walk or less at a run. Llanddwyn (Newborough) Beach, just to the east of the island, is a great place to swim, bordered by forest and extensive dunes and with wonderful views of Snowdonia National Park.

The route: from Newborough Beach car park head straight out onto the beach, turning right and running along the sandy shore towards the rocky outcrops of the island, visible in the distance. At Llanddwyn follow the clear path that heads south-west – one of two main paths that traverse the length of the island. Follow this wonderfully runnable trail, drinking in the sights and sounds all around you until you reach the path's end, a perfect place to stop and enjoy the views. Head back, following the alternative path to the mainland.

Local Highlights

→ Visit Newborough Warren National Nature Reserve, a haven for wildlife including oystercatchers, cormorants and wading birds.
→ For confident paddlers there's some enjoyable kayaking to be found along the length of the Menai Straight; otherwise hire a local guide to take you. There's also an annual Menai Challenge – a time trial along the Straight – (www.performanceseakayak.co.uk).

Back on the main beach, either take the path inland after 300 metres and then head right back to the car park or return via the beach. Please be aware that access to the island is limited during very high tides.

Challenge level: ⭐○○○○
Start/finish: Newborough Beach car park, 1½ miles/2.4km SW of LL61 6SG
Distance: 3½ miles/6km
Map: OS Explorer 263

23 Paddle the Llŷn Peninsula

The Llŷn Peninsula is an Area of Outstanding Natural Beauty – one where the Welsh language and customs are carefully conserved. Its separation from modern, urban life along with its resplendent natural features make it a popular place to visit, particularly for those who love the outdoors life.

Aberdaron lies at the south-western end of the peninsula, a pretty, former fishing village bordered by the wide, sand-edged arc of Aberdaron Bay. Sea kayaking is the way to explore here, with miles of coastline and secret coves to explore. Or take a trip over to Bardsey Island, the legendary 'Island of 20,000 Saints', and see the ruins of St Mary's Abbey, as well as the seals and seabirds, and even dolphins further out to sea. If you're not an experienced sea kayaker there are several local companies offering guiding, tuition and kayak/paddleboard hire. The National Trust, which owns and looks after much of this stretch of coast, has partnered with local company Llŷn Adventures to offer drop-in introductory sessions (chargeable). You can also book guided kayak tours and hire kayaks through them.

Challenge level: ✪✪✪✪
Location: Aberdaron Bay, LL53 8BE
Map: OS Explorer 253

Southern & Central Scotland

The sparsely populated moorland and forest of the Southern Uplands are interspersed by several ranges of hills, ripe for exploration. To the north lie the Central Lowlands, home to 70% of Scotland's population alongside easy access to amazing outdoor adventures. There are two contrasting National Parks here: Loch Lomond and the Trossachs, and the mighty Cairngorms, as well as the secret sandy beaches of Argyll, and, on the opposite side of the country, the Moray Coast. There's something for everyone here, from gentle sightseeing rambles to multi-day epic adventures.

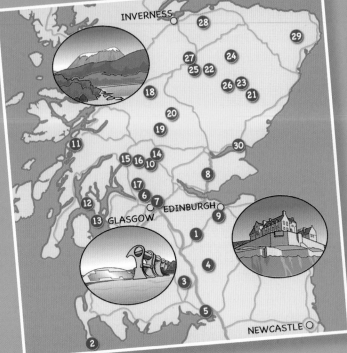

The Borders, Dumfries & Galloway

The Borders are dotted with intriguing historical sites, and the Pennine Way finishes its 267-mile (430km) journey here. To the west lies Dumfries and Galloway with its rocky, sandy coast, lush inland forests and rolling hills. It's a fantastic destination for mountain bikers, and a fine place to spot wildlife.

Around Glasgow & Edinburgh

Glasgow and Edinburgh boast a surprising number of green spaces and the two cities are linked by the Union Canal. Further afield lie wild lochs and coastline, and the lesser-known ranges of the Pentland and Ochil hills.

Argyll

Stretching westwards from Loch Lomond to take in the intricate, island-dotted coastline, Argyll is perfect for those who love water-based adventures. Discover coastal bike rides, sea kayak trails and incredible wild swimming.

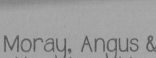

Loch Lomond & the Trossachs

Loch Lomond and the Trossachs National Park covers 720 square miles (1,865 sq km) of mountains, glens and forests. It's a relatively easy area of Scotland to reach from the south, with a diversity of landscapes that lends itself to adventures of all kinds. Loch Lomond itself is 24 miles (39km) long and the largest lake in Britain by surface area, with more than 30 islands dotting the water, great for exploring by kayak or paddleboard. The West Highland Way runs along the eastern shore of the loch, on its 96-mile (154km) route from Glasgow to Fort William.

Moray, Angus & Aberdeenshire

Bottlenose dolphins, seals, porpoises and even orcas are found along this coastline, with its superb sandy beaches, high cliffs and rocky sea stacks. South of the Cairngorms, the gentle Sidlaw Hills make for some enjoyable days out. Within easy reach of the granite city of Aberdeen lie Aberdeen beach, a wide sandy bay, and the Aberdeenshire coast, fantastic for epic endurance challenges as well as for the local wildlife.

The Central Grampians

The Grampians occupy almost half the land area of Scotland and encompass Britain's highest mountains, Ben Nevis in the west and Ben Macdui within the Cairngorm range to the east. The central region is home to Scotland's most remote Munro, Ben Alder, and the vast, windswept wilderness of Rannoch Moor.

The Cairngorms

Home of one of the great mountain writers, Nan Shepherd, and many of the great mountain challenges, five of the UK's six highest mountains and an incredible 55 Munros can be found here. Much of the range lies deep in snow and ice over the winter, but comes alive with wildlife and multi-day adventures in summer.

Bikepack the Tweed Cycleway

Starting in Biggar at 655 feet (200m) above sea level and finishing on the coast in Berwick-upon-Tweed, the Tweed Cycleway is a 95-mile (153km) waymarked cycle route that runs through the heart of the Scottish Borders following the meandering route of the river Tweed. Passing through picturesque countryside and visiting historical sites, the route is almost entirely on quiet roads and makes for an enjoyable ride, whether you're doing it in a day or taking a few days, exploring as you go. There are many glorious views to admire and interesting towns along

Local Highlights

→ Enjoy a well-earned refuel at the Barrels Ale House in Berwick-upon-Tweed, where there's regularly live music in the evenings.

→ Explore the medieval Berwick Castle, a remnant of Anglo-Scottish warfare. The fortifications encircle the whole town – an intriguing circular walk (English Heritage; free entry).

the way, such as Peebles, Melrose, Kelso and Coldstream. The route is undulating, with a few steep sections to challenge the legs. It is normally tackled from west to east, as described, to take advantage of the prevailing winds and the greater overall descent in this direction. The route can also be started in Carstairs (approximately 10 miles/16km from Biggar), where there is a railway station; there is also one at the finish in Berwick.

Cycling is a great way to explore the Borders, and there's a huge number of cycle routes – visit cyclescottishborders.com for lots of information.

Challenge level: ✪✪✪✪✪ if done in a day
Start: Biggar High Street, ML12 6DA
Finish: Berwick-upon-Tweed, TD15 1DG
Distance: 95 miles/153km
Maps: OS Explorer 336, 337, 338, 339 and 346

2 Run the Mull of Galloway Trail

The headland of the Mull of Galloway is Scotland's most southerly point. A long, slender peninsula, like an anchor into the Irish Sea, it is a nature reserve and one of the last remaining sections of natural coastal habitat on the Galloway coast, home to a wide variety of plant and animal species. The Mull of Galloway Trail is one of Scotland's Great Trails, with two sections, one from the Mull to Stranraer and the second from Stranraer along the eastern shore of Loch Ryan to Glenapp. In total the trail is 34 miles (55km) in length, however the main section is a glorious 24-mile (39km) run the full length of the peninsula, hugging the coast the whole way. This is a remote and unspoilt area and the route takes you along high headlands, across sandy bays and through countryside and small settlements. It is waymarked throughout and begins at Robert Stevenson's lighthouse, where there's also a car park. Regular buses connect Stranraer with the Mull of Galloway, making for a great day's adventure starting with a breathtaking run down to the Mull, a refuel with a view at the Gallie Craig Coffee House (www.galliecraig.co.uk), and a scenic bus ride back. Look out for red squirrels,

Local Highlights

➡ Visit the six Gardens of Galloway, Scotland's garden route through an incredible variety of flora growing in the relative warmth of the Gulf Stream (www.scotlandsgardenroute.co.uk).
➡ Immerse yourself in the Galloway wilds at North Rhinns camping (www.northrhinnscamping.co.uk).

deer and seals along the way. There's a railway station at Stranraer, making the whole adventure very achievable by public transport.

If you'd prefer to experience running the Mull of Galloway with company and water stations, there's an annual trail marathon each May.

Challenge level: ✪✪✪✪✪
Start: Mull of Galloway, DG9 9HP
OS grid ref: NX 157303
Finish: Stranraer, DG9 8EJ
OS grid ref: NX 065609
Distance: 24 miles/40km
Map: OS Explorer 309

3 Ride the 7stanes 🌐 🏛

Kirkpatrick Macmillan is generally credited with being the inventor of the pedal bicycle. Born in 1812 in Keir, a small parish in Dumfries and Galloway, and a blacksmith by trade, he was reportedly seen out riding on a 'velocipede of ingenious design', according to a local newspaper. A 1939 plaque on the family smithy in Courthill reads: 'He built better than he knew'.

It therefore seems fitting that this part of Scotland is home to the internationally renowned 7stanes mountain bike centres, all packed with a range of trails of outstanding quality and located in awe-inspiring landscapes managed by the Forestry Commission. Each centre is marked with a 'stane' (Scottish for stone) – a sculpture depicting a local myth or legend – designed by artist Gordon Young. There are, in fact, eight trail centres, as two (Glentress and Innerleithen) share one of the stanes. Access to the trails is free, although there is a car-parking charge if you use the on-site car parks. All the centres have a great range of trails with grades to suit everyone, from green family trails to technical black routes. Here's the full list – can you ride them all?

Maps: OS Explorer 313, 319 and 322

The 7stanes

Forest of Ae – home to the shortest place name in Britain – has two downhill runs, the Shredder, a ¾-mile (1.1km) introduction to downhilling, and the trickier, mile-long Ae Downhill.

Mabie Forest, on the Solway Coast, has an outstanding 12-mile (19km) red route, the Phoenix, with a great mixture of natural trails and singletrack through this picturesque and wildlife-rich forest.

Dalbeattie Forest, also on the Solway Coast, surrounds Plantain Loch, often busy with gulls, ducks, herons and damselflies. The blue-graded Moyle Hill Trail takes you on an 8¾-mile (14km) escape, with fantastic views across the Urr estuary.

Kirroughtree, on the edge of Galloway Forest, has an exhilarating and technical 8¾-mile (14km) black route – Black Craigs – that combines fast-flowing singletrack with technical sections over granite-strewn trails.

Glentrool lies deep in the heart of Galloway Forest. The excellent Big Country Route is an epic 36-mile (58km) adventure taking in minor public roads and forest roads, long climbs and steep descents, along with beautiful views of Galloway's lochs and hills.

Glentress and **Innerleithen** are the most northerly of the 7stanes centres. At Glentress you'll find the world-renowned Red Route: 11 miles (18km) of finely balanced technicality and pure exhilaration. Innerleithen is the place to go for downhill thrills.

Newcastleton lies right on the Anglo-Scottish border and is one of the quietest of the centres. There's a blue-graded family ride and an outstanding red route with 15 miles (24km) of glorious singletrack.

4 Swim Loch Skeen

Located in a remote corner of Dumfries and Galloway, the Grey Mare's Tail waterfall tumbles 200 feet (60m) down the rocky hillside from Loch Skeen into the Moffat water valley. Managed by the National Trust for Scotland, the area is a nature reserve and abundant in wildlife, including a resident herd of wild goats. From the car park on the A708 a steep, winding, rocky path makes its way up the side of the falls, and at the top a

> Where deep deep down, and far within
> Toils with the rocks the roaring linn;
> Then issuing forth one foamy wave,
> And wheeling round the giant's grave
> White as the snowy charger's tail
> Drives down the pass of Moffatdale.
>
> Sir Walter Scott

short stretch of level moorland brings you to the peaceful shores of Loch Skeen, ringed by the craggy plateau. Swim in the clear water (wetsuit recommended) watching peregrines wheeling above. Return by the same route. You can also walk all the way around the loch – a little under 2 miles (3.2km).

Challenge level: ✪✪✪✪✪
Start/finish: Grey Mare's Tail car park on the A708
OS grid ref: NT 186145
Distance: 3 miles/5km
Map: OS Explorer 330

Local Highlights

→ Sleep in well-equipped safari tents or bring your own tent and choose from the walled garden, the woods or wild camping out on the hillside at Wild Woods Camping Ruberslaw (www.ruberslaw.co.uk).
→ Explore the Southern Upland Way and the Annandale Way from nearby Moffat.
→ Refuel at the Gordon Arms in Mountbenger.

131

5 Bikepack the Scottish C2C

Local Highlights

→ Along the C2C at Moffat the Annandale Way starts at Annandale Head. This 53-mile (85km) route makes for a great on-foot adventure, and there's an annual ultramarathon along its length (www.pureChallenge.co.uk).

→ The Ultimate Scottish C2C Guide by Richard Peace is a highly recommended companion guidebook to the route.

→ Owned by David Gray, one of the founders of the Scottish C2C, Chain Events offers a full support service to those undertaking the challenge (www.chain-events.co.uk).

The Scottish C2C is a 125-mile (201km) waymarked cycle route that winds across the Southern Uplands, linking Annan on the Solway Firth with South Queensferry on the Firth of Forth near Edinburgh. The route was conceived by David Gray and John Grimshaw, the cyclists behind the English C2C, along with walking and cycling charity Sustrans. The route takes in a mixture of country lanes, designated cycle paths and seaside promenades. It features two challenging climbs, the first over the classic Devil's Beef Tub and the second through the Moorfoot Hills, before opening out onto a panoramic view of the Lothians, Edinburgh Castle and the Firth of Forth. It finishes under the mighty Forth Rail Bridge.

With a bit of planning it's perfectly possible to ride the Scottish C2C without using a car. The nearest mainline station to the start in Annan is Carlisle, and it's a 21-mile (34km) ride from Carlisle to Annan, where there are plenty of places to stay so you can start fresh in the morning. At the finish it's 11 miles (18km) from Queensferry to the station in Edinburgh.

Challenge level: ✪✪✪✪✪
Start: Annan, DG12 5DY
OS grid ref: NY 192660
Finish: Firth of Forth, Queensferry, EH30 9SQ
OS grid ref: NX 065609
Distance: 125 miles/201km
Maps: OS Explorer 322, 330, 336, 344 and 350

6 Ride the West Highland Way

The West Highland Way runs for 96 miles (154km) between Milngavie, on the outskirts of Glasgow, and Gordon Square in Fort William. The route passes through Mugdock Country Park, skirts the shores of Loch Lomond and the foothills of Ben Lomond, winds through Glen Falloch and Strathfillan, crosses Rannoch Moor and passes Buachaille Etive Mor to the head of Glencoe, climbing the Devil's Staircase and descending to Loch Leven before entering Lairigmor and Glen Nevis, finally finishing at Gordon Square in Fort William.

Designed as a long-distance walking route, it takes most people up to a week to complete it. It is estimated that around 80,000 people use the path every year, of whom over 15,000 walk the entire route. The Way is also popular for running, with several ultramarathons held along it.

In recent years the West Highland Way has also become a popular challenge to cycle, and a two-day completion is achievable by most people with a good level of fitness and good bike-handling skills. Expect to walk plenty of sections, especially those passing under low bridges and following the narrower sections of trail, and also when encountering other trail users, farm animals and wildlife. If you're happy taking it slowly and enjoying the experience rather than aiming for a

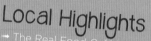

Local Highlights

→ The Real Food Café in Tyndrum is a must-visit for those completing the West Highland Way.

→ The annual West Highland Way race is an ultramarathon that takes in the full distance from Glasgow to Fort William each summer. The 53-mile (85km) Highland Fling is a great introduction, held each spring.

fast time it's a fantastic trail to ride. With the exception of East Loch Lomond, wild camping is permitted on most unenclosed land along the route. Wild camping makes the adventure even more special, but please camp considerately and leave no trace.

Challenge level: ✪✪✪✪✪
Start: Milngavie, Glasgow, G62 6AQ
Finish: Gordon Square, Fort William, G1 1YU
Distance: 96 miles/154km
Maps: OS Explorer OL38, OL39, 348, 377, 384 and 392

133

7 The Glasgow to Edinburgh Canoe Trail

Following the Forth & Clyde Canal and the Union Canal from Pinkston Watersports in Glasgow city centre across the Central Belt to the heart of Edinburgh, the 54-mile (87km) Glasgow to Edinburgh Canoe Trail is a great way to see the cities and the landscapes between them. It's also a brilliant and enjoyable challenge, with relatively safe conditions throughout. There are five portages along the route and also several tunnels – we'd advise taking a red light for the stern of your boat and headtorches so you're visible to oncoming craft when you're travelling through these. Scottish Canals (www.scottishcanals.co.uk) also recommend that you register your trip before departing so that you can be updated with any information relevant to your trip.

The first four portages are short sections around locks; however, the final portage is around the Falkirk Wheel, a distance of around half a mile (900m). There's full information at the Wheel, but a portage trolley is advised to avoid a lengthy carry.

You can paddle the trail in either direction, but west to east takes advantage of the prevailing wind. The following sections make for a 5-day trip, stopping where there are facilities and places to stay: Glasgow to Twechar, Twechar to Falkirk Wheel, Falkirk Wheel to Linlithgow, Linlithgow to Broxburn, Broxburn to Edinburgh.

Challenge level: ✪✪✪✪✪
Start: Canal Bank Street, Glasgow, G4 9XP
OS grid ref: NS 595667
Finish: Edinburgh, EH3 9QD
OS grid ref: NT 246728
Distance: 54 miles/87km
Maps: OS Explorer 342, 349 and 350

Local Highlights

→ Canoe Hire Scotland offers single- or multi-day canoe and kayak hire, guidance on trips and transport throughout Scotland (www.canoehirescotland.co.uk).
→ The towpath alongside the canal is a great route to cycle, walk or run. With lots of places to stop on the way, it's a perfect multi-day adventure, with regular trains running between the two cities to return you to your start point.

134

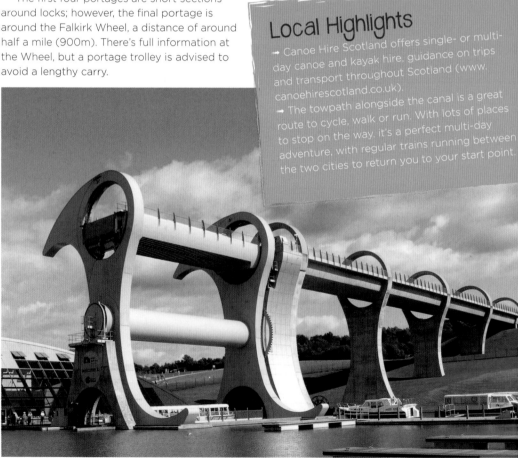

8 Loch Leven Heritage Trail

Loch Leven Heritage Trail is a unique trail linking natural, historical and cultural heritage around Loch Leven. This gentle 12-mile (19km) circuit follows a multi-user path right around the Loch Leven National Nature Reserve, taking you to many beautiful spots on the lochside and through varied woods and marshland. It makes for a wonderfully relaxing run or walk, and a great family-friendly cycle or buggy run. If you're making a day of it, there are several cafés along the route and bike hire is available from the Boathouse Bistro in Kinross.

Set on the southern shore of the loch, the RSPB nature reserve, nationally important for its vast numbers of waterbirds, is great for exploring, although there is an entry fee if you're not an RSPB member. You might spot ospreys here in the summer and pink-footed geese in the winter.

Local Highlights

→ Jump on a boat across to Lochleven Castle, where Mary Queen of Scots was imprisoned during the 16th century (paid entry).
→ East of Loch Leven lie the Lomond Hills, where you'll find some great mountain biking and running trails, as well as the Fife Pilgrim Way, stretching 70 miles (113km) across inland Fife.

Challenge level: ✪✪✩✩✩
Start/finish: Kirkgate Park car park, Kinross
OS grid ref: NO 123019
Distance: 12 miles/19km
Map: OS Explorer 369

9 Carnethy Hill & Scald Law

The Pentland Hills rise from the south-westerly outskirts of Edinburgh and run for about 20 miles (32km) towards the Upper Clydesdale. They're a great place to explore on foot, with over 60 miles (97km) of clear trails across the open moorland tops. This scenic route takes in the highest point of the Pentlands, Scald Law at 1,900 feet (579m), and the picturesque summit of Carnethy Hill, the second highest at 1,880 feet (573m). The main route provides wonderful running on clear switchback paths that wend enticingly up the hillside. The Ranger Centre in Flotterstone is a great source of information on the Pentlands, including the best places to explore and wild camp. There's also a good-sized car park here.

The route: from the Ranger Centre follow signs for Scald Law, climbing up to the summit of Turnhouse Hill before taking to the ridge, following a row of cairns. Continue south-west, climbing over Carnethy Hill and ascending to the summit of Scald Law. Heading left from here, a fun, fast descent leads to the road and house at the head of Loganlea Reservoir. Follow the quiet burn track 3 miles (5km) back to Flotterstone.

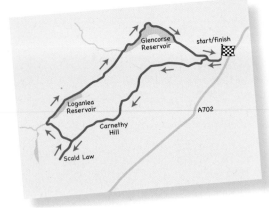

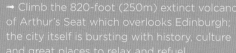

Challenge level: ✪✪✪✩✩
Start/finish: Flotterstone Ranger Centre, Penicuik, EH26 0PR
OS grid ref: NT 232630
Distance: 7½ miles/12km
Map: OS Explorer 344

Local Highlights

→ Try out the local fell racing scene with the Carnethy 5 Hill Race, a classic on the Scottish fell racing calendar, organised by Carnethy Hill Runners.
→ Climb the 820-foot (250m) extinct volcano of Arthur's Seat which overlooks Edinburgh; the city itself is bursting with history, culture and great places to relax and refuel.

10 Ride the Ardgartan Peninsula

Set within Argyll Forest Park, the village of Ardgartan lies on the western shore of Loch Long. There's a delightful 20-mile (32km) waymarked circuit that takes you out around the wild, rugged and remote Ardgartan Peninsula with excellent views of the Clyde and the surrounding mountains. Starting on forest roads, the route climbs up to Corran Lochan, where you'll find some interesting singletrack. There's an enjoyable descent to Lochgoilhead followed by a stretch of quiet road, then it's back onto forest tracks. A long climb followed by an even longer descent brings you back to the start. Maps are available from the Ardgarten Visitor Centre (www.activescotland.org.uk). Further afield in the forest park there are many excellent trails to explore, from woodland and lochside trails to the nearby Arrochar Alps, including the Cobbler (see page 142), and plenty of wild, peaceful swimming spots too.

Local Highlights

→ Refuel at the Three Villages Café (also known as the Pitstop) in Arrochar village, owned and run by the Arrochar Tarbet Community Development Trust.
→ Visit the spectacular Donich Falls – there are several waymarked circular walks from the Visitor Centre.

Challenge level: ★★★☆☆
Start/finish: Ardgartan, Aberfoyle, FK8 3UX
OS grid ref: NN 269037
Distance: 20 miles/32km
Maps: OS Explorer OL37 and OL39

Paddle the Argyll Sea Kayak Trail

The Argyll Sea Kayak Trail runs for over 90 miles (145km) between Ganavan, in the north of the county, and Helensburgh in the south, taking in some of the best sea kayaking in Europe. With its naturally diverse coastline, sheltered waters, islands, sandy beaches, caves and incredible wildlife, it is a perfect place to explore on the water. The trail is designed to make paddling along this spectacular section of coastline as accessible and logistically straightforward as possible, with clear information and guidance on paddling provided. Along the route there are nine access points, as well as the Crinan Canal, with guaranteed parking and trailer storage alongside or nearby. Each of the sections between these points can be paddled individually, or you can join together as many as you wish to make a longer trip. Completing the full distance over a few days, wild camping in between, is an experience no paddler should miss.

There are several companies that lead guided trips along the trail, including ISKGA-approved Sea Kayak Argyll (www. seakayakargyll.co.uk).

Local Highlights
→ Port Ban camping, right on the Kayak Trail at Kilberry, has camping, glamping and an onsite shop, perfect as a base for exploring the trail or as a stopover on your way through.
→ The Argyll Sea Kayak Trail is a project aimed at benefiting the local communities as well as kayakers from all over the world. To help develop the project in the future you can provide feedback on your adventure at www. paddleargyll.org.uk.

Challenge level: ⭐⭐⭐⭐⭐
(full distance)
Start: Ganavan, PA34 5TB
OS grid ref: NM 861325
Finish: Helensburgh, G84 0AD
OS grid ref: NS 239909
Distance: 90 miles/145km
Maps: OS Explorer OL37, OL38, 357, 358, 359 and 362

12 Swim the Secret Coast

Local Highlights

→ The Tarbert–Portavadie ferry runs an hourly service throughout the summer across to Tarbert, where you'll find shops, cafés and restaurants.

→ National Cycle Network Route 78, the Caledonia Way, takes in a loop of the Cowal Peninsula on quiet roads, part of its epic 237-mile (381km) route from Campbeltown to Inverness.

→ Stay at the tranquil, tree-lined Glendaruel campsite at the northern end of the Cowal Peninsula (www.glendaruelcaravanpark.com).

Ostel Bay, also known as Kilbride Bay, lies on the eastern side of the Cowal Peninsula on Argyll's spectacular Secret Coast. This is a place of wild, empty hillsides, pale, sandy crescent bays and clear blue seas.

This part of Argyll is wild and remote, with a rugged, intricate coastline, quiet beaches, hills, glens, sea lochs, clear waters and ancient forests. Edged by the Kyles of Bute and Loch Fyne, it's a great place for exploring by kayak or paddleboard, with lots of wildlife to spot and plenty of pretty villages and welcoming pubs.

There are no facilities or parking at Ostel Bay, but you do often have the wide, sandy crescent all to yourself, or perhaps there'll be a few others there on a sunny day, with uninterrupted views out to Arran. To find it, take the B800 from Tighnabruaich and Kames to the crossroads at the village of Millhouse. Turn left towards Ardlamont and follow the single-track road (with passing places) for a few miles until you reach a parking lay-by just past Kilbride Farm (OS grid ref: NR 96103 68215).

Challenge level: ✪✪✪✪✪
Location: Ostel Bay (Kilbride Bay),
Ardlamont, Argyll, PA21 2AH
OS grid ref: NR 959667
Map: OS Explorer 362

13 The West Island Way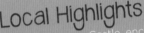

The Isle of Bute lies in the Firth of Clyde, just off mainland Scotland. At 15 miles (24km) long by 4 miles (6.4km) wide it has just one town – Rothesay – which is linked by daily ferries to Wemyss Bay, a 40-minute drive or train ride from Glasgow. Lying along the Highland Boundary Fault, the northern half of the island is rugged, hilly and extensively forested, whereas the southern half is lower-lying and more cultivated. The island is an eclectic mixture, with ageing Victorian splendour and Scottish wilderness a backdrop to chic hotels and eco-renovations. The 30-mile (50km) West Island Way was the first waymarked long-distance walk on a Scottish island and it's a great way to explore. It runs the complete length of the island with a loop at either end, crossing a dramatic landscape, with a beautiful coastline, beaches, farmland, moorland and forests. If you're up for a challenge you could run it in a day, or walk it in two or more – for the full Bute experience, take a tent and wild camp along the way.

Challenge level: ●●●○○

Start: Kilchattan Bay, PA20 9NG
OS grid ref: NS 108544
Finish: Port Bannatyne, PA20 0LT
OS grid ref: NS 069673
Distance: 30 miles/50km
Map: OS Explorer 362

Local Highlights

→ Visit Rothesay Castle, encircled by a sandstone wall and associated with the Stewart kings of Scotland. The four towers were added after the Norse siege of 1263. Stay at the Rothesay Castle View Apartment (aviewlessordinary.com).
→ Refuel at the quirky Ettrick Bay Tearoom.
→ Swim, sail, kayak or simply watch the sun set over the beautiful, peaceful Kyles of Bute.

14 Cycle Loch Katrine ⊕

The long, ribbon-like stretch of Loch Katrine lies in the very heart of the Trossachs, immortalised by the poetry of Sir Walter Scott. The circular cycle route that links it with Loch Ard takes in 35 challenging but beautifully enjoyable miles – and you could always combine it with our Loch Ard swim (see page 143) for a great weekend of adventures. There are some steep climbs

(see page 143)

Local Highlights

→ The Trossachs Boulders, above the south-east basin of Loch Katrine, are a great venue for boulderers. The rock is rough-textured mica schist, on which there's a wide range of problems of all grades, with good landings.

→ Sleep at one of the well-furnished eco lodges, right at the edge of Loch Katrine, perfectly placed for stargazing (www.lochkatrine.com).

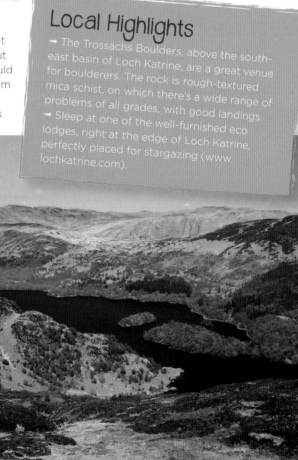

through Achray Forest and some remote sections where you'll need to be confident at basic bike repairs to avoid a long walk should you run into trouble. Cycle hire is available from Katrine Wheelz at Trossachs Pier (summer only) and Go Country in Kinlochard.

The route: head north out of Aberfoyle on National Cycle Network Route 7, at first on road and then heading through Queen Elizabeth Forest Park. The route takes you past picturesque Loch Drunkie – keep an eye out for red squirrels, and even ospreys in the summer months. Just past Loch Drunkie bear left, leaving Route 7 and heading westwards along the southern shore of Loch Achray (caution: road crossing at the A821). Just

after the Achray Hotel take the road signed 'Loch Katrine' to reach the visitor centre. From there there's a scenic tour of the loch on very quiet tarmac trail – the landscape here is breathtaking. Finally join public roads through peaceful Loch Ard Forest to return to Aberfoyle.

Challenge level: ✪✪✪✫✫
Start/finish: Trossachs Discovery Centre, Aberfoyle Main Street, Stirling, FK8 3UQ
Distance: 35 miles/56km
Map: OS Explorer OL38

15 Climb the Cobbler 🏛 ✳

The Cobbler – also known as Ben Arthur/Beinn Artair – has the most distinctive outline of any mountain in the Southern Highlands. Rising to 2,900 feet (884m), it has three separate summits, with the central, rocky pillar being the highest. The mountain has been used as a training ground by rock climbers since the late 19th century and holds an important place in climbing history. For those with sure feet and a good head for heights, the final moves up to the true summit first involve 'threading the needle' – squeezing through a hole in the rock face to reach the rocky, stepped climb to the top. This is a popular mountain for good reason, combining pleasant walking up the recently improved path with an exhilarating finish. Although exposed, the final section is a straightforward scramble and the summit is reached via large hand and foot holds; however, it is an altogether different prospect in very wet or windy conditions or in the winter.

The route: from the car park in the village of Succoth, at the head of Loch Long, cross the road and follow occasional waymarkers to ascend the wide zigzagging path through the trees, the height soon bringing great views down to the loch and across to Ben Lomond. Keep straight ahead, passing a dam, until the three peaks of the Cobbler come into view ahead. Continue following the main path, crossing several streams on stepping stones, until you reach the Narnain boulders, used as shelters by climbers in the past. At Lochan a' Chlaidheimh (OS grid ref: NN262066) turn left at the path junction and ascend the stone steps, following the clear path to the summits.

Challenge level: ✪✪✪✪✩
Start/finish: Succoth village car park, G83 7AP
OS grid ref: NN 294049
Distance: 7½ miles/12km (out and back on same route)
Map: OS Explorer OL39

Local Highlights

→ Shore Cottage, perched on the picturesque shores of Loch Fyne, in Strachur, is a perfect place to base yourself for adventures both within the National Park and further west on the Argyll coast. There's also a shop and post office nearby, and you're right on the Ardgartan mountain bike route (page 137).

16 Swim Loch Ard

Loch Ard lies a few miles west of Aberfoyle in Queen Elizabeth Forest Park and is considered to be the source of the river Forth, which flows from here to the Firth of Forth at Edinburgh. The loch is a wonderful swimming spot: very sheltered, 3 miles (5km) long and not as cold as some of the deeper lochs – although a wetsuit can still be a good idea. There are four islands on Loch Ard: Eilean Gorm; Briedach; St Mallo, which is rumoured to have an old chapel dedicated to that saint; and Dundochill, which is the site of Duke Murdoch's castle that may have been built by the Duke of Albany. All of them are fun to explore from the water, whether you're swimming or exploring by boat. The best entry points are from parking lay-bys on the main Aberfoyle to Stronachlachar road – one is on the opposite shore to Rob Roy's cave, just round from Helen's Point, and the other is near the water sports centre further up the road.

There's a wonderful network of trails through the surrounding forest, perfect for exploring on foot or bike and with plenty of interesting wildlife to spot too, including roe deer, barn owls and capercaillie. Vigour Events holds an annual swim festival here, with distances from 1km to 12.5km (www.vigourevents.com).

Local Highlights

→ Explore the forest by bike – family-friendly trails run alongside Loch Ard, and others head deep into the trees.

→ Climb the 2,392-foot (729m) peak of Ben Venue from nearby Loch Achray car park for breathtaking views of the National Park.

→ Enjoy a post-swim refuel at the excellent Ailean Chraggan pub in nearby Weem, just outside Aberfeldy.

Challenge level: ★★★☆☆
Location: Loch Ard, FK8 3TF
OS grid ref: NN 463019
Map: OS Explorer OL46

17 The Three Lochs Way

The Three Lochs Way is one of Scotland's Great Trails, a 34-mile (55km) linear route through the Loch Lomond & the Trossachs National Park. Waymarked throughout, it links Loch Lomond, Gare Loch and Loch Long in four stages, with a railway station at the start and end of each section, except at Inveruglas at the very end, where there's a bus stop. It can of course be undertaken in one go, or over two days, with plenty of opportunities for a wild camp along the way.

A great way to see the less-visited side of Loch Lomond, the route begins at Balloch, gateway to the National Park, and crosses the moors to reach Helensburgh. It passes through Garelochhead and Arrochar before the final stretch through the hills to Inveruglas on Loch Lomond. The return trip up the eastern shore of Loch Lomond can be done by linking with the West Highland Way at Inveruglas.

Local Highlights

→ Wild camping is restricted in some areas around Loch Lomond; however, Cashel Campsite, right on the eastern shores of the loch with stunning mountain views, is a great pace to base yourself. There's easy access for swimming and kayaking; to the winding trails to explore around Queen Elizabeth Country Park with; and to the mountains beyond (www.campingintheforest.co.uk).

Challenge level: ✪✪✪✩✩
Start: Balloch station, G83 8SS
OS grid ref: NS 389818
Finish: Inveruglas, G83 7DW
OS grid ref: NN 323098
Distance: 34 miles/55km
Maps: OS Explorer OL37, OL38 and OL39

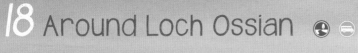

Local Highlights

→ Hike out to Ben Alder and stay at the remote, recently renovated bothy, Ben Alder Cottage (www.mountainbothies.org.uk).
→ Follow the West Highland Way across Rannoch Moor, one of the highest, wildest parts of the trail.

Loch Ossian lies on the Corrour Estate on the north-eastern edge of Rannoch Moor, a shining, 3-mile-long (5km) sliver of water against a backdrop of high mountains. Part of the joy of visiting here is its remote location with no road access – Corrour station, where several trains a day will stop by request, is just a short distance away.

The inviting 9-mile (14km) trail that loops all the way around Loch Ossian makes a great adventure in its own right, or as part of a longer stay exploring the area around Ben Alder, Scotland's most remote Munro. It is also possible as a day trip from Glasgow – the Caledonian Sleeper stops at Corrour by request. Camp out in the wilds, away from everything, or stay at SYHA Loch Ossian, a recently renovated eco-hostel powered by the sun and wind. An early-morning run, followed by a dip in the loch, is one of the best ways we can think of to start the day.

Challenge level: ✪✪✪✩✩
Start/finish: Corrour station, PH30 4AA
OS grid ref: NN 356664
Distance: 9 miles/14km
Map: OS Explorer 385

19 Paddle Loch Tay

Some 2,500 years ago, people lived on Loch Tay, on artificial islands called crannogs. Most of the loch's eighteen crannogs are now submerged; however, you can still see one near the northern shore at Kenmore.

Loch Tay is the largest loch in Perthshire, and one of the deepest in Scotland. It's a magnificent dark stretch of water, 15 miles (24km) long and around 508ft (155m) deep. To the north rise the impressive mountains of Ben Lawers National Nature Reserve, and National Cycle Network Route 7 runs along the quiet southern shore.

Paddling the length of the loch, or simply exploring around it and visiting the small island at its western end, is a great way to spend the day, and there are plenty of wild camping spots along the quieter sections of shoreline. There are two main launch points: Killin Castle and Firbush. Both are at the far western end of the loch, with parking for a few cars at each. If you don't have your own boat there are several hire centres – Killin Outdoor Centre on Main Street in Killin has a good selection and you can launch straight into the river Lochay, which flows into Loch Tay.

Local Highlights

→ Climb the brilliant Ben Lawers – park on the minor road off the A827 between Loch Tay and Lochan na Lairige (OS grid ref: NN 609376) and follow the clear path north-east to the summit at 3,983 feet (1,214m). Out and back is about 6½ miles (10.5km) in total.

→ Refuel at MacGregor's Market in Killin – an organic café plus community shop and information centre.

Challenge level: ★★☆☆☆
Location: Main St, Killin, FK21 8UJ
Map: OS Explorer OL48

Glen Lyon is the longest enclosed glen in Scotland, stretching for over 30 miles (50km) from the village of Fortingall in the east to Loch Lyon in the west. It was once described by Sir Walter Scott as the 'longest, loneliest and loveliest glen in Scotland'. The river Lyon snakes its way along the flat bottom of the glen, in places in wide, shallow meanders, in others gushing through corries and gorges. There are pools perfect for a swim near Bridge of Balgie, with parking and a tearoom nearby, and further on there are the remote lochs of Loch Lyon and Loch an Daimh.

The route: from Fortingall church head west out of the village and turn right onto the twisting single-track road that runs through the glen. The road is initially hemmed in by high mountains and hugs the wooded banks of the river Lyon but soon opens out towards the hamlet of Innerwick, from where footpaths lead up into the hills for sensational views up and down the glen. At Bridge of Balgie you'll find a tearoom, popular with walkers and

Local Highlights

➡ Take in the fascinating history of Fortingall village, starting with the Fortingall Yew, which may be at least 5,000 years old (some sources claim the figure is nearer to 9,000) and is perhaps the oldest tree in Europe. Nearby there are the remains of ancient Caledonian forest, ruined castles and a deep chasm known as MacGregor's Leap where, in 1565, the chief of the Clan MacGregor reputedly escaped a group of pursuing Campbells.

cyclists for many years.

From here, a road runs on for another 11 miles (18km), ending at the huge dam of Loch Lyon, one of the most remote but most beautiful places in Scotland. Return by the same route.

Challenge level: ✪✪✪✩✩
Start/finish: Fortingall village church, PH15 2LL
Distance: 40 miles/66km
Map: OS Explorer OL48

21 Glen Esk Waterfalls

Glen Esk is the longest and most easterly glen in Angus, and Mount Keen, far up the valley, is Scotland's most easterly Munro. The route down the glen makes a great run, the steep sides channelling you along, with a stretch right at the edge of Loch Lee and a climb up past tumbling waterfalls. It takes you all the way around Craig Maskeldie before an enjoyable climb over the top of Cairn Lick brings you to an all-out exhilarating descent that zigzags back to the valley floor. On a hot day the finishing stretch back along the loch just has to be swum. The river North Esk rises here and flows south through green and tranquil Glen Esk to reach the North Sea near Montrose. Further downstream, just north of the pretty village of Edzell, the North Esk falls through a rocky gorge at the wonderfully named Rocks of Solitude. The walk from the village up to the falls and back is beautiful.

Challenge level: ✪✪✪✩✩
Start/finish: Invermark car park, Glen Esk, DD9 7YZ
Distance: 10 miles/16km
Map: OS Explorer OL54

Local Highlights

➡ Described as the jewel in the crown of Angus, Edzell village is an interesting place to explore. Through the Dalhousie Arch at the entrance to the village, the long, wide and ruler-straight main street is lined with Victorian buildings, neat hedges and many tearooms. There's even a ruined 16th-century castle with a walled garden.

Ben Macdui

start/finish — Ski Centre

1141 Cairn

Stob Coire an t-Sneachda

Lochan Buidhe

Ben Macdui

Local Highlights

→ CairnGorm Mountain centre is home to Britain's highest funicular railway and offers guided excursions into the mountains – skiing over the winter months (www. cairngormmountain.org).

→ If you're adventuring with a group take a look at Inshriach House: perfectly positioned on the edge of the Cairngorms near to Aviemore, it sleeps up to 17 self-catering. The River Spey runs past the house, perfect for swimming, and there's a 200-acre estate to explore. Inspired glamping options also available (www.inshriachhouse.com).

At 4,295 feet (1,309m), Ben Macdui is the second-highest mountain in Britain after Ben Nevis, and the highest in the Cairngorm range. There are many routes to its summit, varying in length, difficulty and steepness, but on a clear day every one of them will reward you with incredible 360-degree views from the top.

The most straightforward ascent of Ben Macdui is from the Coire Cas car park at the ski centre, which, at 2,130 feet (650m), launches you deep into the Cairngorm plateau. Although this takes some of the trudge out of the initial ascent and there are no technical aspects to the route, you'll still need good mountain navigation skills to complete it. The entire route is above the tree line, through a bare, rocky moonscape. Look out for only the hardiest of birds: ptarmigans, dotterels, snow buntings and golden eagles.

The route: from the start head south up the Fiacaill of Coire Cas to reach the big cairn at 3,743 feet (1,141m). Follow the rim of Coire an t-Sneachda on your right until you reach its lowest point. At the top of Coire Domhain, pick up a path climbing gently for a few hundred metres. Contour round to the little Lochan Buidhe, the highest body of water in the British Isles.

Follow the path 1½ miles (2km) south to the summit of Ben Macdui, with its rocky cairn topped by a trig point. To return, retrace your steps to Lochan Buidhe and head north-west along the edge of the Lairig Ghru. Climb over the shoulder of Cairn Lochan to reach a high open step before continuing north down the ridge to the west of Coire Lochan. Rejoin your outward path back to the car park. NB: do not attempt in poor visibility or winter conditions without the expert knowledge and specialist equipment necessary.

Challenge level: ✪✪✪✪✪
Start/finish: Coire Cas car park, Cairngorm Ski Centre, PH22 1RB
Distance: 11 miles/17km
Map: OS Explorer OL57

23 Lochnagar & Loch Muick

Meaning 'small loch of laughter', Lochnagar is the highest and finest mountain in the Mounth, a range in the south-eastern Cairngorms. It's a popular ascent and paths are generally clear and well maintained; however, as with all the higher tops, poor weather can make for extreme conditions. Choose a clear day and reaching the summit ridge is an experience never to be forgotten; in 1849 Lochnagar was climbed by Queen Victoria, who described it as 'one of the wildest, grandest things imaginable'.

> Away, ye gay landscapes, ye gardens of roses,
> In you let the minions of luxury rove,
> Restore me the rocks where the snow-flake reposes,
> Though still they are sacred to freedom and love.
> Yet Caledonia, beloved are thy mountains,
> Round their white summits though elements war,
> Though cataracts foam 'stead of smooth-flowing fountains,
> I sigh for the valley of dark Lochnagar.
>
> Lord Byron

From Spittal of Glenmuick, head south-west along a track to reach the north-eastern tip of Loch Muick. Turn right here and cross a footbridge, following the path along the lake's northern shore. Nearing the far end of the lake you'll reach a wooded area and pier. From here you can either continue around the loch – a full circumnavigation is an enjoyable run/cycle of just under 8 miles (13km) – or turn right to head to the summit of Lochnagar. The path ascends steeply and follows the long groove of Glas Allt north-west on clear paths to reach the top of the Corrie of Lochnagar, where steep cliffs drop dramatically to the loch far below. Carefully avoid the cliff edge, keeping it to your right and aiming for the Cac Carn Mor cairn before continuing straight ahead to the summit of Lochnagar at NO 243861.

Local Highlights

→ Visit Braemar Castle, built in the 17th century, overlooking the River Dee. It's had a varied and tumultuous past and is rife with myths and legends (www.braemarcastle.co.uk).

→ Braemar Mountain Festival celebrates the best of mountain adventure and culture annually in March (www.braemarmountainfestival.com).

Challenge level: up to ✪✪✪✪✪
Start/finish: Spittal of Glenmuick, AB35 5SU
OS grid ref: NO 309851
Distance: circumnavigation of Loch Muick is 7¾ miles (12.5km), additional 4 miles (6.4km) each way to the summit of Lochnagar and back
Map: OS Explorer OL53

24 Ride Glenlivet

Glenlivet Estate is part of the Crown Estate and covers 58,000 acres of the Cairngorms National Park. It's a glorious mixture of wild and managed, with mountains,

Wild camping is permitted on the Glenlivet Estate but please don't light fires or pitch near to roads or buildings. There's also a range of accommodation on the estate, from hotels to a campsite, along with cafés and restaurants. Entry and parking are free.

Local Highlights

→ When in the Highlands... Take a trip to the Glenlivet Distillery, open during the summer, to see whisky being made, and even sample a drop.

→ Trail maps of the estate are available online should you want to plan your adventure in advance (www.glenlivetestate.co.uk).

Challenge level: varies
Location: Glenlivet Estate,
Tomintoul, Ballindalloch, AB37 9EX
Map: OS Explorer OL58

moorland and rivers, outstanding purpose-built mountain biking trails, over 20 different waymarked routes for walking or running, and plenty to keep families happy too. Over half of the 14-mile (23km) Red Trail is singletrack, with a predominately smooth surface. Aside from this you'll find forest road, tough climbs and technical features (all avoidable), all set against a spectacular backdrop. If you'd prefer to find your own way, there are miles and miles of trails across the estate – take a map and go exploring. On-site facilities for cyclists include a bike wash (free), a shop with bike spares, a pump track, bike hire and a café serving great coffee – heaven.

25 Explore the Caledonian Rainforest

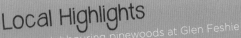

Many consider Rothiemurchus to be one of the finest examples of a Caledonian pine forest in Scotland. It's a special place – described by David Attenborough as 'one of the glories of wild Scotland' – and was owned by the Grant family for 500 years before being sold in 2014 to the Forestry Commission, which now manages it carefully to preserve this precious piece of the country's history.

A temperate rainforest by definition, this is a unique environment in which species found nowhere else in the British Isles breed. These include the western capercaillie, the common goldeneye, the European crested tit, the parrot crossbill and the Scottish crossbill.

Local Highlights
➝ The neighbouring pinewoods at Glen Feshie are also well worth a visit.
➝ Camp within the forest at the excellent Rothiemurchus campsite (www.campandcaravan.com).
➝ The estate farm shop sells everything you need for a perfect picnic.

Loch an Eilein lies hidden deep within the forest, a small, peaceful loch with an island topped with a ruined 15th-century castle. There's a lovely walk around the edge of the loch, and a network of trails leads off into the wider estate to be explored, either on foot or by bike. Bike hire is available from the Rothiemurchus Centre on site.

Challenge level: ✪✪✩✩✩
Location: Loch an Eilein car park, PH22 1QT
OS grid ref: NH 897085
Map: OS Explorer OL57

Local Highlights

→ Glenmore Lodge offers a vast range of expert-guided outdoor adventures, including mountain biking, climbing, kayaking and skiing (glenmorelodge.org.uk).
→ The local mountain race takes on Lairig Ghru, traversing the 43km between the police stations at Aviemore and Braemar. Held annually in June, it raises funds for the Cairngorm Mountain Rescue Team.

Two parallel glaciated valleys run north–south across the Cairngorm plateau, linking Speyside with Deeside. To the west is Lairig Ghru – an ancient drovers' road that rises to 2,740 feet (835m), taking in some truly wild and remote sections and passing below the western slopes of Ben Macdui – a tough but classic crossing. To the east is Lairig an Laoigh, a lesser-known and gentler path following Glen Derry and winding through pinewoods and over bleak moorlands. There are several river crossings that may be impassable after heavy rain, so time your trip carefully.

A full circuit making a double crossing of the Cairngorms using these two historical routes is an outstanding, challenging adventure. At around 18 miles (30km) a day, you could do it over a weekend if you're running/fastpacking, with a night at the outdoor centre at Glenmore Lodge. Or walk it with a lightweight tent and wild camp along the way for a more relaxed exploration of the area.

The routes: both routes run north–south between Glenmore Lodge and Linn of Dee, and the circuit can be started and finished at either end. Buses run to Aviemore, where there's a railway station.

Challenge level: ✪✪✪✪✪
Start/finish: Glenmore Lodge, Aviemore, PH22 1QZ
OS grid ref: NH 986094
or Linn of Dee, AB35 5YG
OS grid ref: NO 062897
Distance: 18 miles/29km each way or 36 miles/58km round trip
Maps: OS Explorer OL57 and OL58

27 The Speyside Way

One of four official Long Distance Routes in Scotland, the 65-mile (105km) Speyside Way follows the Spey Valley from Aviemore in the northern Cairngorms to the Moray Firth at Spey Bay. It then continues a short distance eastwards along the coast to Buckie. It is a truly epic walk from the mountains to the sea (or from the sea to the mountains), with many wonderful spots along the way for swimming in the ever-present Spey and wild camping on its peaceful shores. For this very reason we'd recommend not attempting it during the peak of the midge season – July and August.

The official guide breaks the distance down into eight stages based on the primary towns and villages along the way: Buckie – Spey Bay – Fochabers – Craigellachie – Ballindalloch – Grantown – Nethy Bridge – Boat of Garten – Aviemore. It also works very well to arrive at the towns at lunchtime and spend the nights in the tranquillity of the countryside.

Challenge level: ✪✪✪✪✪
Start: Aviemore station, PH22 1PD
Finish: Harbour Head, Buckie, Scotland, AB56 1XR
Distance: 65 miles/105km
Maps: OS Explorer OL57, OL60, OL61 and 424

Local Highlights

→ Towards the end of the Speyside Way at Spey Bay, 5 miles (8km) short of Buckie, is the Scottish Dolphin Centre and wildlife reserve, a fascinating place to spend a day.
→ Ride the Moray Monster Trails at Fochabers, 20km of excellent singletrack.
→ Run the Speyside Way Race, held in August each year over 36½ miles (59km) of the trail (www.speysidewayrace.co.uk).

155

One of the longest rivers in Scotland, the Findhorn rises in the Monadhliath Mountains and flows through Moray forests and countryside, reaching the sea at the beautiful Findhorn Bay, famous for its biennial arts festival. The eco-village of Findhorn and the nearby Findhorn Foundation are fascinating to visit, along with the wildlife-rich Culbin Forest.

The exciting, changeable nature of the Findhorn River makes it a fantastic destination for watersports; it's a renowned white water kayaking venue, and stretches are also popular for canyoning, jumping and rafting – there are many slides, chutes and falls along its rocky, winding course. Between the busy spots, however, you'll find long stretches of deep, calm water, stained tea-coloured by the peaty tannins that give the local whisky its distinctive flavours.

To find the best swimming spots, go to the Logie Steading Visitor Centre, where there's also a café and farm shop. Daltulich Bridge and Randolph's Leap with its narrow, rocky chasm are great places to start – but please be aware these are also access points for kayaks. Another great spot for a swim is the beach at OS grid ref NJ 001500, just downstream of the Findhorn's confluence with the river Divie.

Local Highlights

➤ Camp or glamp at Ace Hideaways (www. acehideaways.co.uk) – there's canyoning, white water rafting, kayaking and cliff jumping available to book on site.

➤ Walk or cycle the Dava Way, 24 miles (39km) of off-road path that follows the course of the Findhorn.

➤ Explore the Logie Estate with its great walks, shops, cafés and heritage centre.

Challenge level: varies
Location: Logie Estate, Forres, Moray, IV36 2QN
Maps: OS Explorer OL61 and 423

29 Paddle the Ythan

The river Ythan rises at Wells of Ythan near the village of Ythanwells and flows 37 miles (60km) south-eastwards through Aberdeenshire to reach the sea near Newborough. Although it has been known to flood the surrounding areas following heavy rain, the rest of the time it is a wonderfully gentle river to paddle with calm water and high, grassy banks. There are a few islands around Ellon to navigate, but this only adds a little more interest. The Ythan Estuary, the lower reaches of the river, is a Special Protection Area, being a breeding ground for three species of tern.

You can get out either at the Kirkton of Logie Buchan Bridge or at the bridge at Newborough in the estuary, although this second option is exposed and tidal. Please also be considerate of anglers as this is prime fishing territory. How far up you start from depends on how long you have – from Methlick it's about a 10-mile (16km) paddle, but the stretch from Fyvie is also delightful, adding another 8 miles (13km). Above here it gets a little small.

Challenge level: ⚫⚫⚫⚪⚪
Start: Methlick, AB41 7DT
OS grid ref: NJ 857372
Finish: Ythan Estuary, Newburgh, Ellon, AB41 6BY
OS grid ref: NK 002247
Distance: 10 miles/16km
Maps: OS Explorer 421 and 426

Local Highlights

→ Camp at the wonderful Ythan Valley Campsite in Ellon, complete with organic bread, free-range eggs and a bush shower... (www.ythanangling.net).
→ The Redgarth pub in nearby Oldmeldrum serves fantastic local ales and whisky from the village distillery.

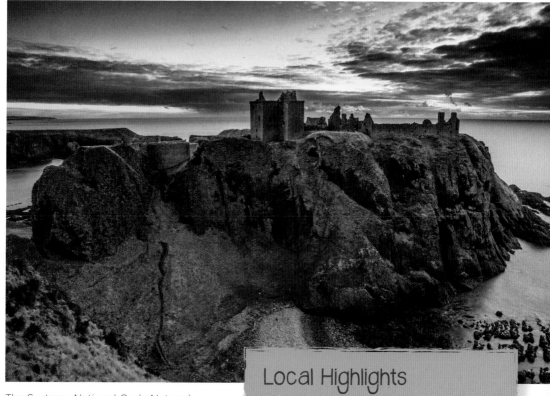

Local Highlights

→ Award-winning Arbroath smokies from Iain R Spink have made the town famous, and with good reason (www.arbroathsmokies.net). Smokies are served alongside many other traditional Scottish dishes at The But'n'Ben restaurant in Auchmithie, 3 miles (5km) north of Arbroath.

The Sustrans National Cycle Network Route 1 runs from Dover to Shetland, 1,695 miles (2,728km) along Britain's east coast. The 172-mile (277km) section between Edinburgh and Aberdeen is also known as the Coasts and Castles route, as it passes several sites of historical interest. Beginning in Edinburgh, it crosses the Firth of Forth into the Kingdom of Fife and then follows the coast north, passing Dunnottar Castle, and ending in Aberdeen. This stretch also forms part of the North Sea Cycle Route, an absolutely epic circumnavigation of the coasts of all the countries bordering the North Sea: Belgium, the Netherlands, Germany, Denmark, Sweden, Norway, England and Scotland – over 3,800 miles (6,120km) of cycling.

The Coasts and Castles route between Dundee and Arbroath is an enjoyable, flat, mainly traffic-free cycle along the Tay Estuary. It begins under the Tay Road Bridge – bring photographic ID to get through the docks – and passes through Broughty Ferry to Monifieth. Traffic-free trails lead over Barry Links to Carnoustie, finishing at Arbroath's historic harbour.

Challenge level: ⭐⭐✩✩✩
Start: under the Tay Road Bridge, Dundee, DD1 4BY
Finish: Arbroath harbour, DD11 1TD
Distance: 19 miles/30.5km
Maps: Coast & Castles North, AA Cycling in Scotland, OS Explorer 380 and 382

Deep in the north of Scotland, the mountains get higher, the glens deeper and the rivers wilder. Summer evenings go on for ever, but then so can the rain. Winter is harsh and unforgiving, often lingering long into the year. Long lochs reflect the mood of the sky: joyful blue or grey as granite. There's a beautiful melancholy here, one that sparks the fire of creativity and adventure.

Lochaber

One of the great outdoor capitals of Britain, Lochaber is home to Ben Nevis, the highest mountain in the UK; Glencoe; and the sandy beaches and green landscapes of the Road to the Isles. It also boasts Ardnamurchan, the most westerly point in the British Isles.

The Great Glen & the North-East

The 62-mile (100km) Great Glen is a huge rift valley spanned by several lochs connected by rivers. Loch Ness is undoubtedly the most famous, both for its resident mythical monster and for being huge, containing more water than all the lakes in England and Wales combined.

The North-West

Wild, rugged, spectacular, remote, inspiring, the north-west Highlands are adventurer heaven, with the pale, sandy crescents of the beaches, the rugged mountains that rise from lush, forested glens, the intricate coastline and the rivers that carve through the landscape. This area has also been designated a Geopark by UNESCO in an effort to preserve the unique character of this truly special place.

The Far North

Tucked into the far north-west corner of Scotland, the landscape around Assynt is truly extraordinary. From a vast, undulating moorland, steep-sided mountains rise incongruously from the edges of lochs. The coastline here is spectacular, with rugged cliffs, remote sandy beaches and rocky sea stacks; it's a great place to watch dolphins and whales too.

Paddle Loch Sunart

The Ardnamurchan peninsula is a wild, remote yet beautiful part of the west coast of Scotland. This special area is unspoilt and undisturbed, with a remoteness that makes it feel more like an island. The landscape is surprisingly varied – forest, moorland and hills dotted with many lochs, and then the spectacular coastline scalloped with sandy beaches. Look out for golden eagles soaring high above the trees and for whales and dolphins out in the bays. Loch Sunart, the longest sea loch in Scotland, dominates the western end of the peninsula – it's 19 miles (31km) long with a number of islands along its length. The largest of these, the 600-acre Carna, has two self-catering properties on it where you can stay and explore the loch at your own pace. The loch is a haven for wildlife and a Marine Protected Area for its rare flame shell beds. Look out for otters too.

The islands of Carna, Oronsay and the petite Risga sit inside the shelter of Loch Sunart and are a relatively easy paddle and wonderful to explore. Heading out into the Irish sea allows you to reach Mull, Coll and Tiree, but these trips are a serious undertaking and require plenty of experience and knowledge of the area. Arisaig Sea Kayak Centre (arisaigseakayakcentre.co.uk) is a local company offering a range of trips with qualified, experienced guides.

Challenge level: ★★★☆☆
Location: Loch Sunart, Ardnamurchan, Lochaber, PH36 4HZ
Maps: OS Explorer 383 and 390

Local Highlights
→ Stay at Ardnamurchan Campsite and Study Centre (www.ardnamurchanstudycentre.co.uk) basic but beautifully positioned, and has internet access.
→ Visit Ardnamurchan Lighthouse – which also has a café.
→ Stay on the island of Carna in a self-catering cottage, boat included (www.isleofcarna. co.uk).

2 Explore Knoydart

The Knoydart peninsula is an extraordinary place. Cut off from the UK mainland road network, it is only accessible by boat or on foot. Much of Knoydart is owned and managed by the Knoydart Foundation, a community-run organisation that looks after this special place and its people.

The landscape here is remote, rugged and beautiful, with some challenging mountains along its length, Ladhar Bheinn being the highest point at 3,346 feet (1,020m). The main settlement on Knoydart is the village of Inverie, home to around 120 residents. Here you'll find the shops, café and pub, and also the pier for access by boat to the peninsula. You're not allowed to bring cars onto Knoydart, so arrival is either by a 2-day walk with a wild camp – definitely an amazing adventure in its own right – or by ferry from Mallaig. There is a station at Mallaig, so you can travel there by public transport.

There are many wonderful trails to explore by bike – if you don't take your own, bike hire is available from Knoydart Carbon Cycle, which has a fleet of top-notch steeds for adults and children. Inverie woods has a challenging downhill mountain bike trail, and lots of gentler options too. The three Munros on the peninsula (Ladhar Bheinn, Luinne Bheinn and Meall Buidhe) are all challenging but enjoyable walks, and the views across Knoydart to the Skye Cuillins are worth the climb. The sandy beaches edged by clear blue seas make Knoydart one of the best places in Britain for swimming too; if you're lucky, you'll be joined by otters. A great way to experience Knoydart is with an experienced guide. Steven Fallon (www.stevenfallon.co.uk) comes highly recommended.

Challenge level: various
Location: Mallaig, Knoydart, PH41 4RH
Map: OS Explorer 413

Local Highlights

→ Pick your own produce from the Community Market Garden, east of Inverie Bay. There's a snack bar there several days a week too.
→ Stay at the Knoydart Foundation campsite at Long Beach – and wake up to some of the best views in Britain.
→ Discover the Road's End Café in Airor and watch seals, otters and herons at Airor Bay.

3 Ben Nevis by the Carn Mor Dearg arête

Local Highlights

➡ Stay at Great Glen Yurts in Torlundy, waking up to views of Ben Nevis (www. greatglenyurts.com).
➡ Visit the Ben Nevis Inn, a converted barn at the start of the mountain path right at the foot of the Ben – the inn serves food and there's also a bunkhouse (www.ben-nevis-inn.co.uk).

Considered to be among the best ridge walks in the country, the Carn Mor Dearg (CMD) arête is somewhere between a technically challenging walk and an easy scramble. This magnificent curving line connects two Munros, its rocky ridgeline taking you to airy positions with stunning views of the cliffs of Ben Nevis; however, there's very little ground that requires a hands-on approach. If you're considering climbing Ben Nevis but want a route to the top that's engaging, inspiring and absolutely an adventure, this is for you. Compared with the popular Mountain Track, it's in a different league.

The route: from North Face car park near Torlundy, follow the main track, taking the right turn signed 'Allt a' Mhuillin'. Keep left at the next two forks and then turn left at a junction signed 'Allt a' Mhuillin'. At the next track junction turn right, to stunning views of the Ben. Continue climbing, leaving the forest and heading towards the north face of Ben Nevis. At the next junction turn left up a boggy path towards Carn Mor Dearg. The graceful, curving ridgeline around to the Ben is obvious from here in good weather. Continue up the path, crossing the southern slopes of the mountain before gaining the ridge itself. Follow this until you suddenly find yourself at the summit, usually surrounded by the crowds who have ascended the Mountain Track. The descent is initially via the Mountain Track – in poor visibility navigate carefully between Gardyloo Gully and Five Finger Gully, following a bearing of 231 degrees for 490 feet (150m), and then a bearing of 281 degrees, to pass the most dangerous section. After the zigzags, at OS grid ref NN 147724, turn right off the main path and follow it to the northern tip of Lochan Meall an t-Suidhe. From here descend steeply on vague paths north-east to join your outward path and return to the start. Described for summer conditions only.

Challenge level: ✪✪✪✪✪
Start/finish: Ben Nevis North Face car park, Torlundy, PH33 6SW
OS grid ref: NN 145764
Distance: 11 miles/17.5km
Map: OS Explorer 392

4 Ride Fort William

Home of the UCI Mountain Bike World Cup, Fort William has to be the most famous downhill mountian biking venue in Britain. At the Nevis Range Mountain Experience you can take a test run on the famous downhill course, graded orange extreme. If you're after something a bit gentler but still a thrilling ride, there's the Red Giant XC course. Both of these courses begin at the Gondola, at over 1,970 feet (600m), and there's a charge for the uplift to get you there.

Further down in the forested foothills, but still offering outstanding riding, are the Witch's Trails. There's the family-friendly 4½-mile (7.1km) Broomstick Blue that follows the river Lundy along winding singletrack; the 5¼-mile (8.5km) red-graded Witch's World Champs, built for the 2007 World

Local Highlights
→ Camp or go self-catering at the excellent Glen Nevis campsite, a perfect adventure base (www.glen-nevis.co.uk).
→ Over the winter there's skiing and snowboarding from the ski centre (www.nevisrange.co.uk).

Championships, with plenty of technical features and nearly 900 feet (270m) of climbing; the 6¼-mile (10km) red-graded 10 Under the Ben, 6¼ miles (10km) of singletrack and forest road; plus the affectionately named 'Nessie', a fast and furious snaking descent. There are also the Cat's Eyes and Blue Adder XC descent routes. It's free to ride the Witch's Trails, but there is a charge for parking.

Challenge level: various
Location: Nevis Range Ski Centre, Fort William, PH33 6SQ
Map: OS Explorer 392

164

5 Swim to Morar Bay ⊛ ⊛

The Silver Sands of Morar, a series of beautiful white sand beaches with fine views out to Skye, Eigg and Rum, dot the coastline between Arisaig and Morar, and a walk – or swimrun – along this extraordinary trail is a must. The river Morar, which links Loch Morar with the sea, is one of Scotland's shortest rivers, at around half a mile (0.8km) long, and its lower reaches make for a fine access point to the bay.

Park at the designated parking area on the B8008 at Morar Beach, where the estuary makes a wide sweep edged by fine white sand. Get in here and swim downstream towards the sea, exploring the inlets and coves as you go. The final section takes you out into the sea at breathtaking Morar Bay, from where you can spend the day exploring the rest of the Silver Sands.

Challenge level: ✪✪✪✩✩
Location: Morar Beach car park, PH39 4NT
OS grid ref: NM 675921
Map: OS Explorer 398

Local Highlights

→ Stay at the Camusdarach campsite (www.camusdarach.co.uk), with superb views and direct access to the beaches.
→ Pick up a picnic from the Ardshealach Smokehouse in nearby Glenuig.
→ Hop on a ferry from Arisaig to go island hopping around the Small Isles.

Local Highlights

→ Paddle the Great Glen Canoe Trail as a 5-day holiday with great company and experienced guides through Wilderness Scotland (www.wildernessscotland.com).
→ Explore Loch Ness and the atmospheric ruins of Urquhart Castle which stood proud at the water's edge through 500 years of conflict.

The Great Glen Canoe Trail follows the route of the Caledonian Canal along the Great Glen for over 60 miles (97km) and is Scotland's first official canoeing trail. Running from Fort William to Inverness, there are 22 miles (35km) of paddling on canal and the rest is across the series of lochs, exploring these incredible bodies of wildlife-rich water from within. There are several portages along the route which you'll need to negotiate, but they are all straightforward. The trip is generally broken down into five sections, with stops where there are easy exit/launch spots and facilities; five days also makes a nice length of time to paddle, with a day or two at either end for arrival and departure. The sections are: Fort William – Gairlochy – Loch Oich – Foyers – Dochgarroch – Inverness. You can, of course, paddle it in fewer sections, but if you do, we'd recommend running official sections together for logistical simplicity. Register with Scottish Canals for a free licence to paddle before you set out. There are several hire and guiding companies in the area.

Challenge level: ✪✪✪✪✪
Start: Lochy Bridge, Fort William, PH33 6TJ
Finish: Inverness station, IV1 1LF
Distance: 62 miles/100km
Maps: OS Explorer 392, 400 and 416

7 Bikepack the Great Glen Way

Aside from the shortest route between Fort William and Inverness – straight down the middle along the water – there are also two other ways of traversing the Great Glen. The walking route begins at the end of the West Highland Way, so it's a popular extension for those who want to see more of Scotland. There's also an outstanding 73-mile (118km) cycling route, waymarked throughout, that, unusually for a long-distance trail, is only suitable for mountain bikes. It takes in much of the higher ground along the Glen, climbing through pinewoods where deer graze peacefully between the trees, and descending steeply to discover interesting settlements. It's also a sociable route, popular with cyclists and also coinciding with the walking trail at times, and you meet plenty of locals too. It is all these features making it completely and utterly different from the Great Glen Canoe Trail that earn it a separate listing here. Were it not between the same towns, you'd rarely know you were on the same stretch of the country.

You can, of course, simply turn up with your bike at either Fort William or Inverness and set out on the trail. There are several options for overnight stops – most three-day itineraries break at Fort Augustus on the first night and at Drumnadrochit on the second – or you could go for it in one. You could also bikepack the trail, complete with camping kit, stopping for a wild camp wherever you choose. Ticket to Ride (www.tickettoridehighlands.co.uk) offers one-way bike hire and guiding, while Wilderness Scotland (www.wildernessscotland.com) offers a 5-day guided tour of the area, including a full crossing of the Great Glen.

Challenge level: ✪✪✪✪✪
Start: Fort William station, PH33 6TQ
Finish: Inverness station, IV1 1LF
Distance: 73 miles/118km
Maps: OS Explorer 392, 400 and 416

Local Highlights

→ Eat, sleep and enjoy a warm welcome, whatever the weather, at Abriachan Eco-Campsite & Café. Located at the highest inhabited croft in Scotland it is open every day all year round.

→ The Velocity Café and Bicycle Workshop in Inverness is a social enterprise 'working to promote healthy, happy lifestyles through cycling' and well worth a visit for a bicyclatte, or a campagcinno (velocitylove.co.uk).

8 The Falls of Orrin

The river Orrin rises in the East Monar Forest and winds its way east through the Strathconon and Corriehallie forests to its confluence with the river Conon, 5 miles (8km) south-west of Dingwall. Just to the west of Muir of Ord are the Falls of Orrin, a delightful, tumbling series of waterfalls in a secluded wooded area. You'll often spot salmon leaping here – in fact it is said that the record for the highest leap by a salmon was set here, at over 11 feet (3.5m). There is space to park just off the road on the south side of the river at Aultgowrie, just before the bridge. From here it is a short walk upstream to the falls, and above the falls there are wide pools for swimming, with a shingle beach for access. The pool and river below the falls have some great spots too, and a little further downstream is a shingly area perfect for paddling. There's a wonderful walk that takes in the falls and the nearby ruins of Fairburn Tower, starting at the car park and

heading upstream as far as Stronachroe. Cross at the bridge here and follow the river back down the other side, through pretty woodland back to the falls. Fairburn Tower is just north of the falls from here, or cross back over the road bridge at Aultgowrie.

Challenge level: ●●●○○
Location: Aultgowrie, IV6 7XA
OS grid ref: NH 476514
Map: OS Explorer 431

Local Highlights

➡ Visit the nearby village of Muir of Ord, where you'll find the Glen Ord distillery.
➡ Stop for picnic provisions at Black Isle Berries at Ryefield Farm, Tore – you'll find a range of locally sourced produce, as well as pick-your-own berries.
➡ Pitch up at the Loch Ness Shores Camping & Caravanning Club site (non-members welcome), an eco-friendly site on the peaceful southern shores of the loch, set in spectacular surroundings. Also a great stopover along the Great Glen Way.

9 Ride the Black Isle

The Black Isle isn't really an island at all. It's a peninsula, bounded on three sides by water – the Cromarty Firth to the north, the Beauly Firth to the south, and the Moray Firth to the east. This is a place of wild coastal landscapes and rolling hills, dotted with forests and castles, and networked with tracks, trails and quiet roads to explore. It is named for its contrast with the surrounding areas in winter when snow doesn't lie here so it looks black against the surrounding white highlands. On the southern side of the Black Isle, Chanonry Point is a great place to see dolphins.

Cycling is the way to get around here and there are trails everywhere, from quiet rides exploring the villages and breweries to the more technical off-road trails.

The 26-mile (42km) Beauly Firth Loop is mostly on road, but it's a perfect way to explore the south of the Black Isle. Starting at Inverness, it follows a waymarked loop along the banks of the firth, visiting the villages of Beauly and Muir of Ord before taking in the full southern coast of the Black Isle to North Kessock, finishing with the bridge back across to Inverness. Look out for seals and dolphins as you go – and did we mention the breweries?

Local Highlights

➡ The Black Isle Brewery makes craft organic beer and the results are excellent. As well as a shop there's a wood-fired pizza oven and 14 en-suite rooms, and they're open all year (www.blackislebrewery.com).

➡ Head to Learnie Red Rock Mountain Bike Trail Centre where you'll find three purpose-built waymarked trails with something to suit every level of rider.

Challenge level: ★★☆☆☆
Start/finish: Inverness station, IV1 1LF
Distance: 26 miles/42km
Map: OS Explorer 432

Loch Maree lies in Wester Ross just north of Torridon. It is 12 miles (19km) long and 4 miles (6.4km) wide, making it the largest freshwater loch north of Loch Ness. Loch Maree is scattered with densely wooded islands, the remnants of ancient Caledonian pine forests. There are over 60 islands in total, with five larger

Local Highlights

→ Considered to be one of the least polluted bodies of fresh water in the country, Loch Maree is a wonderful place for a swim. It's a straightforward swim out to the islands and a great way to visit them – but the loch is cold and deep, so a wetsuit is recommended.

→ Visit Beinn Eighe National Nature Reserve on the south-eastern edge of the loch. Good paths lead up past waterfalls to the viewpoint and cairn at around 1,800 feet (550m) (OS grid ref: NG 993632) – there are also a couple of stunning remote lochs here to explore.

→ Refuel at the unique Badachro Inn on Loch Gairloch (badachroinn.filmdesign.org.uk).

ones, including Isle Maree, which was once inhabited and has the remains of a chapel and a graveyard on it. The largest of the islands, Eilean Subhain, has a lochan within it, and on this lochan is an island, the only such arrangement known to exist in the UK.

This is an internationally important area for wildlife, and Beinn Eighe, on its southern shores, is the UK's oldest National Nature Reserve. One of the best ways to explore the loch and its islands is by kayak or paddleboard, and a trip out to wind your way between the green-topped islets is a great way to spend a day. Many of the islands have restrictions at certain times of the year, so

check locally before landing on any of them; you could start at the Loch Maree Hotel, but please don't park here without asking permission. The parking area at Slattadale is a good place to put in. Wilderness Scotland (www.wildernessscotland.com) will take you out for an expert-guided paddle on the loch, but be aware that midges can be very bad during July/August.

Challenge level: ✪✪✪✩✩
Location: Loch Maree, Gairloch, IV22 2HL
OS grid ref: NG 929716
Map: OS Explorer 433

Traverse the Glen Shiel Ridge ✵

The glorious Glen Shiel Ridge rises and falls across a 9-mile (14.4km) stretch of the Highlands between Loch Cluanie in the south-east and Loch Duich in the north-west. One of the absolute classic walks in this part of the country, it follows an airy line, with the occasional bit of easy scrambling, over no less than seven Munros. At nearly 17 miles (27km), it's a good day's walk, and a few hours of running, but it's well worth it. This is a linear route, so you'll need to arrange transport back along the A87 through Glen Shiel.

The route: start by following the old private road between Cluanie and Tomdoun, which you can reach just east of the Cluanie Inn. Continue along this, zigzagging up to the summit of Creag a' Mhaim. The ridge and path from here are clear and fairly straightforward to follow in good conditions,

climbing to the summit of each Munro and descending between them. After the final summit, Creag nan Damh (hard work at

Local Highlights

→ Stay at Shiel Lodge on the Glenshiel Estate. Sleeping up to 16 it's the perfect base for exploring the area and stands overlooking the River Shiel and at the head of Loch Duich, home to the ruined 13th-century Eilean Donan Castle (www.glenshielestate.com).
→ The Five Sisters of Kintail is another classic walk in this area, taking in the six(!) Munros on the opposite site of the glen.

this point), follow a vague path marked by cairns as it winds down the northern slope, following the western bank of Allt Mhalagain. Cross a footbridge at the bottom to return you to the A87, about 6 miles (9.6km) from your start point.

Challenge level: ✪✪✪✪✪
Start: Cluanie Inn, Glenmoriston, IV63 7YW
Finish: Glen Shiel
OS grid ref: NG 970139
Map: OS Explorer 414

[Map]

finish
Shiel Bridge
A87
start
Cluanie Inn
Creag nan Damh
Creag a' Mhaim

A Torridon Weekend

The Torridon Hills, a spectacular jagged range, rise to the north of Glen Torridon, with exhilarating walking and scrambling leading to their high summits and ridges. Perhaps the best known of these mountains is Liathach, whose twin peaks rise gracefully from the glen, offering splendid views of the surrounding hills and across to Skye. An ascent of Liathach is reason enough to visit this beautiful part of Scotland; however, there are some excellent, and quite different, adventures to be had further along the Glen too. On reaching Loch Torridon by car, turn right onto a minor road that skirts the northern shore of the lake.

Local Highlights

→ As an alternative to the bothy there's a campsite at Torridon village, as well as the shop and café.
→ You can also approach Craig Bothy from the north. Both the Tigh an Eilean Hotel in Shieldaig and the Badachro Inn on Loch Gairloch are well worth a visit.
→ WildBike run guided rides and mountain biking holidays in Torridon and across Britain (www.wildbike.co.uk).

Continue along this road as it turns inland and climbs steeply. At OS grid ref NG 806603 you will come to a small double loch – the second of which is Loch a' Mhullaich. Easily accessible from the road on its northern shore, this is a fine loch for a swim. Afterwards, carry on along the road until it ends at Lower Diabaig, where you'll need to leave your car. Continue on foot along a well-maintained footpath to Craig Bothy (OS grid ref: NG 774638), a former youth hostel that can comfortably sleep six. Further on from here, at Red Point, there are two spectacular sandy beaches, also

perfect for exploring and swimming. Torridon Stores and Café in Torridon village (www.torridonstoresandcafe.co.uk) is open Monday to Saturday in summer and on selected days in winter.

Challenge level: various
Location: Torridon village, IV22 2EZ
OS grid ref: NG 897563
Maps: OS Explorer 428, 429 and 433

13 Cycle the Bealach Mor circuit

A classic ride on the cyclosportive calendar, organised by Hands On Events (www.handsonevents.co.uk), this 90-mile (145km) circuit crosses the famous mountain pass Bealach na Bà to Applecross and is considered one of the toughest circular road routes in the country. The biggest road climb in the UK, it takes in 2,054 feet (626m) of climbing in just 10km of road. Though the climb is leg-sapping, the outstanding views and the feeling of accomplishment at the top are well worth the effort. The organised sportive takes place each September, but you can, of course, test yourself on this infamous route at any time.

The route: Kinlochewe – A832 east to Achnasheen – right to Lochcarron via the A890 – descend through Kishorn – turn right over the bridge. Seven miles (11km) of climbing followed by long descent into Applecross village. Go around Applecross Bay, following the edge of the peninsula to picturesque Shieldaig. Follow the southern shore of Loch Torridon before the final stretch through Glen Torridon to Kinlochewe.

Challenge level: ✪✪✪✪✪
Start/finish: Kinlochewe, Achnasheen, IV22 2PB
Distance: 90 miles/145km
Maps: OS Explorer 428, 429, 430, 433, 435 and 436

Local Highlights

→ The Applecross peninsula lies between the mountains of the mainland and the Isle of Skye. It's a sparsely populated and remote place with wild open landscapes and a spectacular rugged coastline. Camp at Applecross Campsite, sample local delicacies from Applecross Ices and the Smokehouse and enjoy the incredible running, wildlife-watching, kayaking and swimming all around the peninsula.

14 Discover the Old Man of Stoer

The Old Man of Stoer is a towering 200-foot (60m) sea stack of Torridonian sandstone, once a rocky archway across to the mainland, but now a tall, thin island. Rising from the waves in the Minch, just off the Assynt coast, the stack is a popular climbing venue. A Tyrolean traverse is required to reach it, and if there's not one in place when you get there, then someone has to swim out to the stack first. Other than to note that it's an incredible place to climb, with several superb routes for the mid-to-high-grade trad climber, it is well beyond the scope of this book to go into details. There is, however, a wonderful loop to walk – or run – that takes in the Old Man and the nearby countryside.

The route: from Stoer Head Lighthouse, follow signed path to the Old Man of Stoer, ascending steadily on good, runnable tracks alongside the rugged coast with spectacular views emerging all around. Continue north-east along the coast to reach the Point of Stoer. Return south across the rugged lowlands of Sidhean Mor, with fine views of the Sutherland coast and mountains of Assynt. Follow paths past a ruined WWII radar station back to start.

Challenge level: ★✩✩✩✩
Start/finish: Stoer Head Lighthouse car park, 1 mile (1.6km) W of IV27 4JH
OS grid ref: NC 004327
Distance: 4½ miles/7km
Map: OS Explorer 442

Local Highlights
➥ Visit Hermit's Castle, Achmelvich, reputedly the smallest castle in Europe, built in the 1950s and now derelict.
➥ Cycle on the quiet roads, taking in the incredible scenery, or head off-road on the Kyle of Sutherland mountain bike trails.
➥ Wake up to views of white sand and blue sea at Clachtoll Beach campsite (www.clachtollbeachcampsite.co.uk).

15 Surf John o' Groats

When it comes to the best of British surf spots, most people think of Cornwall or Pembrokeshire. But some of the country's best surf can be found about as far away on the British mainland as it's possible to get from the South-West. It's a shame that most people only go to John o' Groats to start (or finish) a journey between there and Land's End, some 870+ miles (1,400+km) south, for the surf there rivals any to be found elsewhere on the UK coast.

Dunnet Bay, between Thurso and John o' Groats, is a 3-mile (4.8km) stretch of beach with waves that break the whole way along. It's a great spot for less experienced surfers and bodyboarders as there are plenty of places along its length with smaller swells. If you're more experienced, head just west of here to Thurso East – considered one of the best places for surfing in Europe. Summer is a great time for beginners as the swell is smaller and the conditions less variable. Although the air's cooler later in the year, the sea temperature can still be reasonable and the surf gets

Local Highlights

→ Visit Dunnet Head, the most northerly point in mainland Britain.
→ Sample some of the local gin or vodka at Dunnet Bay Distillery.
→ Warm up in the Storehouse Café, with views out to Orkney.
→ Relax in style after a day out on the waves at Natural Retreats John o' Groats, a stylish collection of self-catering spaces (www.naturalretreats.co.uk).

bigger and more consistent, so if you're after bigger waves you might want to head there in the autumn. For much of the year you will still need a good-quality wetsuit and neoprene boots, gloves and hood.

Challenge level: various
Location: Dunnet Bay, KW14 8XD
OS grid ref: ND 213699
Map: OS Explorer 451

16 Bothy at Sandwood Bay

The final stretch of the Cape Wrath Trail crosses remote Sandwood Bay en route to Cape Wrath, the end of its 205-mile (330km) journey north from Fort William. The mile-long (1.6km) stretch of the bay, owned by the John Muir Trust, is often considered to be one of the best beaches in Britain, and with its remoteness and relative inaccessibility, meaning there are never crowds of sunbathers, it's definitely up there. To reach Sandwood Bay, begin in the John Muir Trust car park at Blairmore and follow the well-used track north-east past several lochans and Sandwood Loch to reach the beach.

Not far from the beach is Strathchailleach bothy, a tiny shelter that makes for a fascinating visit or overnight stay. Until 1996 this was the home of James McRory Smith, known locally as Sandy, who lived there for 32 years with no mains electricity, running water or telephone, and with the nearest buildings six miles (nearly 10km) away. He lived a simple,

reclusive life and the bothy's walls still bear the murals he left there.

To reach the bothy, walk the length of the beach to reach the Strathchailleach burn at the north-eastern end. Follow the southern bank of this all the way to the bothy.

Challenge level: ✪✪✪✩✩
Start: John Muir car park, Blairmore, IV27 4RU
OS grid ref: NC 194600
Finish: Strathchailleach Bothy, Sandwood
OS grid ref: NC 248657
Distance: 6 miles/10km
Map: OS Explorer 44

Local Highlights

➡ A mile (1.6km) south-west of Sandwood Bay, Am Buachaille rises straight from the sea, a stack of Torridonian sandstone some 200 feet (65m) tall. It was first climbed in 1968.
➡ The Kinlochbervie Hotel is popular with locals and visitors (www.kinlochberviehotel.com).

17 Climb Ben Hope

At 3,041 feet (927m), Ben Hope is the most northerly of all Scotland's Munros. It's a wonderfully isolated mountain, standing alone and with its obvious challenge rising as a pleasingly pointed summit straight from the start. From the car park beside the minor road that follows the river Strathmore, follow the signs for 'Ben Hope Path' uphill on the south-eastern bank of the burn, Allt a' Mhuiseil. The route is unrelenting, climbing up and up, dodging crags and waterfalls and steepening to where it reaches the mountain's western ridge. Follow the ridge north on a clear path, finally reaching the trig point on the rocky summit plateau, to be rewarded by an astonishing panorama. Descent is by the same

Challenge level: ✪✪✪✪✩
Start/finish: roadside car park, 8 miles/13km S of A838/Altnaharra road junction
OS grid ref: NC 461476
Distance: 4½ miles/7.5km
Map: OS Explorer 447

Local Highlights

➡ Stay in Strabeg bothy, a short walk from parking at NC393538. A farmhouse-style bothy, it has plenty of space, and the surrounding mountains await exploration. There's no running water, but there is a small stream next door.
➡ Experienced guide Steven Fallon offers guided excursions on and around Ben Hope, and further afield (www.stevenfallon.co.uk).

path, with some care. A short extension can be added by continuing along the escarpment of Leitir Mhuiseil to reach the waterfall above Alltnacaillich before descending to the road.

The Scottish Islands

The coast around Scotland is dotted with over 790 islands. They vary greatly in size and terrain, each with its own distinct character.

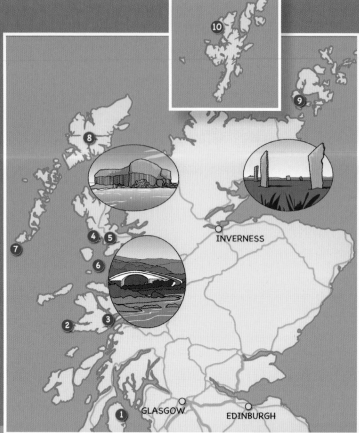

Arran & the Inner Hebrides

Arran, in the south-west, lies just off the coast of Ayrshire, nestled within the Firth of Clyde. North of Arran the Inner Hebrides stretch from Islay in the south up to Skye – the largest and best known – in the north.

The Outer Hebrides, Orkney & Shetland

Flung further out into the Atlantic, the Outer Hebrides, also known as the Western Isles, include Lewis and Harris, North Uist, Benbecula, South Uist and Barra. To the north, the island archipelagos of Orkney and Shetland lie 10 miles (16km) and 90 miles (145km) respectively off the coast of mainland Scotland. With around 20,000 people living on each, they are wildlife-rich and a joy to visit, with friendly communities, beautiful landscapes and a fascinating culture.

Scramble Goatfell ✷

Goatfell is the highest point on Arran at 2,866 feet (873.5m). Its prominent pyramidal peak rises out of the forested hills, an inviting sight as you approach Brodick on the boat. There are several ways to ascend the mountain, with the most straightforward – and popular – being up the south-eastern slopes from Brodick Castle. Our choice, however, is a classic and most enjoyable scramble up the mountain's north ridge. Airy and absorbing, it requires a good head for heights, but the trickiest sections of scrambling can be avoided.

The route: from Corrie, follow signs to Goatfell up a lane west of the A841, taking the path on the right also signed 'Goatfell'. Climb steeply to reach the lower slopes of Coire Lan. Continue on the path to reach the ridge between North Goatfell and Mullach Buidhe and head left here, ascending to the summit of North Goatfell, with some easy scrambling towards the top. From here, head south, descending and gaining the long, fine ridge across to the main summit, or if you prefer not to tackle the scramble you can

walk the path to the east of the ridge. From the summit descend east, keeping straight on when the main path heads right towards Brodick, to rejoin your outward path and return to Corrie.

Challenge level: ✪✪✪✪✪
Start/finish: Corrie, Arran, KA27 8JB
OS grid ref: NS 026421
Distance: 5 miles/8km
Map: OS Explorer 361

Local Highlights

➡ Stay in a stunning yurt near Kilmory (www.runacharainn.com) or pitch your tent at the foot of the mountains at Lochranza (www.arran-campsite.com).
➡ Arran is great for cycling: head to the forest trails for excellent mountain biking or enjoy the 60-mile (97km) circular route around the island on quiet roads.

2 Paddle Mull

Local Highlights

→ You won't want to sleep anywhere other than right next to the beach, beneath the stars at Fidden Farm; nearby Fionnphort has a shop and café.

→ Visit the incredible Fingal's Cave on the nearby uninhabited island of Staffa, formed from hexagonally jointed basalt columns.

With its 300 miles (480km) of coastline, Mull is a prime destination for anyone with a love of the sea. It's a perfect place to start out sea kayaking and paddleboarding too, with sheltered coves and plenty to explore. Fidden Farm campsite on the Isle of Mull has, without a doubt, the best position of any campsite anywhere. It is a wide, grassy expanse overlooking a rugged coastline with secluded sandy coves calling out to be explored. There's a wide, boulder-strewn beach nearby, and dolphins and seals play in the waves while sea eagles soar overhead. It's a perfect base for adventures on, and around, the island. You can launch kayaks and paddleboards straight from the site and go paddling along the coast, keeping in to the sheltered bays, or explore the many rocky islets all within view of the campsite. You can also paddle across to Iona, a straightforward trip in good weather, landing on a white sandy beach and heading off to explore the abbey. You can hire kayaks from Mull Kayaks (www.redburnmull.com/mull-kayaks.html).

The waters around Mull are the best place in the UK to spot whales. Minke whales are the most common here, though you can also see orcas, as well as dolphins, porpoises and basking sharks.

Challenge level: ⭐⭐⭐☆☆
Location: Knockvologan Road, Nr Fionnphort, Isle of Mull, PA66 6BN
Map: OS Explorer 373

Local Highlights

➡ The Keel Row restaurant in Fionnphort is excellent and serves good, traditional food.
➡ Mull is an outstanding destination for wildlife-watching. Look out for orcas, basking sharks, otters, red deer, seals, eagles and a vast array of water, moorland and woodland birds.

Tomsleibhe bothy on the beautiful island of Mull feels wonderfully remote but is easy to reach by bike or on foot. There's track all the way, making it a particularly good spot to visit on a mountain bike, with some great exploring to do around the bothy too. It's a large bothy, sleeping 10, and can comfortably accommodate two parties. If it's full you can wild camp nearby. There are large areas of forest near the bothy, and the river Forsa runs through the glen to its east. Loch Ba, just to the west of the bothy, is a prime spot for spotting sea eagles, and there's a path for most of the length around the loch. Beinn Talaidh, at 2,497 feet (761m), is only a short walk away, and worth the tough climb to the summit for the views.

Craignure in Mull is a 46-minute ferry ride from Oban with Caledonian MacBrayne Ferries (CalMac) (bikes go free). From here the A849 north will take you around the coastal road to Salen, where you'll find the nearest café and restaurant to the bothy (both good). There's also a well-stocked shop here. To reach the

bothy, take the track south off the A849 at Pennygown, just east of Salen. From here it's an enjoyable 4-mile (6.4km) ride following the river Forsa – there are some rougher sections of track nearer the end. At OS grid ref NM 616377 there's a footbridge and the track forks – the right-hand fork is signposted to Tomsleibhe bothy (www.mountainbothies.org.uk).

Challenge level: ★★★☆☆
Start: Craignure, Mull, PA65 6AY
Finish: Tomsleibhe bothy
OS grid ref: NM 617372
Distance: 4 miles/6.4km from the A849.
Craignure to Salen is 11 miles/17.7km
Map: OS Explorer 375

4 Climb Coire Lagan

The traverse of the Black Cuillin on Skye is one of the great mountain running challenges, and a testing day out for even the most experienced walker. Although the ridge itself is only 7 miles (11.2km) long, it's a continuous series of peaks and troughs connected by airy ridges. Most people take 15–20 hours to complete the ridge; however, the current record for running it stands at just under three hours, by local doctor Finlay Wild.

For a taste of the Cuillin with a lot less commitment, there is a great route on fine paved paths through stunning scenery that takes you from the campsite at Glenbrittle right into the heart of Coire Lagan, a great rocky amphitheatre bordered by towering gabbro crags, including the famous Inaccessible Pinnacle, part of the classic Cuillin Ridge traverse.

The route: from the campsite take the path as it climbs eastwards into Coire Lagan. Continue east-north-east along the path, looping clockwise around the tiny loch that lies in the hollow at the base of Sgurr Mhic Choinnich. Return along the path west to the base of the coire, joining the equally spectacular north-west path along the north side of Loch an Fhir-bhallaich to Glenbrittle.

Challenge level: ✪✪✫✫✫
Start/finish: Glenbrittle campsite, IV47 8TA
OS grid ref: NG 408206
Distance: 5½ miles/9km
Map: OS Explorer 411

Local Highlights

➡ The wonderful, crystal-clear Allt Coir' a' Mhadaidh pools and waterfalls are nearby, perfect for a post-hike swim.
➡ The large blocks that lie around the Allt Coire Lagan burn provide some outstanding bouldering, in a stunning setting.

5 Mountain bike Skye ⊕ 🏛

Skye is a fantastic place to mountain bike, with miles of trails looping the island. There's so much to explore here, and much of it's well suited to two wheels. A great starter route takes in some of the tough climbs and exhilarating descents that characterise the riding here. There's a visit to the eerie, abandoned village of Boreraig, which was brutally evacuated during the clearances.

Local Highlights

→ Another great way to explore Skye is by kayak. The calm lochs are perfect for a gentle day's paddling or for beginners, while the intricate coastline is fascinating in a sea kayak. Local company Skyak offers courses and guided paddles (www.skyakadventures.com).
→ Bike hire available from Skye Bike Shack (www.skyebikeshack.com).

The route: from the beach, head to the public road and turn right past Loch Cill Chriosd. Turn right after the church and climb steeply on a narrowing track. From the top descend to the sea and Boreraig. Head west and cross the stream via the stones. Follow the coast path, pushing where you need to as there are some steep and rocky sections. On reaching the top, pause, catch your breath and take in the views. It's all fast singletrack/doubletrack from here back to the beach.

Challenge level: ⭐⭐⭐⭐☆
Start/finish: Camas Malag beach, Skye
OS grid ref: NG 582193
Distance: 11 miles/17.5km
Map: OS Explorer 411

Loch Cill Chriosd

🏁 start/finish

Beinn Bhuidhe

Boreraig

Rubha Suisnish

6 Climb An Sgurr

The Isle of Eigg is an amazing place, owned and managed by the Isle of Eigg Heritage Trust since the community buyout of 1997 and considered to be the most eco-friendly island in Britain. At its centre rises the great volcanic peak of An Sgurr, which has a challenging but enjoyable climb to the summit. The route is straightforward, although lower down the ground is boggy and towards the summit there is some steep and rocky ground. The views from the top are fantastic. There is a shop and tearoom at the pier, where the ascent begins.

The route: from the ferry pier take the road uphill into the woods. Continue straight on through a gate and field, with An Sgurr visible ahead. Follow the track to a gate, turning left through Grulin, an abandoned settlement. At the small cairn, follow the red waymarker right, continuing up the hill towards the impressive peak, following waymarkers – this section can be boggy. Part way along the bottom of the cliff the path heads up through a groove; follow markers along the ridge to the summit. Return is by the outward route. Local guides Laraine and Owain at Eigg Adventures (www.

eiggadventures.co.uk) provide bike hire, kayak hire, guided walking, sailing trips and archery sessions.

Caledonian MacBrayne Ferries (CalMac) run daily services from Mallaig to Eigg.

Challenge level: ✪✪✪✪✪
Start/finish: Eigg ferry pier, PH42 4RP
OS grid ref: NM 484838
Distance: 5 miles/8km
Map: OS Explorer 397

7 Bikepack the Hebridean Way

The Hebridean Way cycle route crosses 10 islands, using ferries and causeways to hop between them. Starting on the Island of Vatersay at the southern tip of the archipelago, it ends 150 miles (241km) later at the Butt of Lewis Lighthouse in the far north. The route is waymarked throughout its length as National Cycle Network Route 780.

The cycling is straightforward and mostly follows quiet single-track roads. You'll discover amazing sights throughout: mountains, moorland, forest, dunes, the Callanish Standing Stones, the sounds of the sea, birds of prey wheeling in the air, corncrakes croaking and, at the end of every day, the sun sinking beyond the Atlantic.

The route: Vatersay – Barra – Eriskay – South Uist – Benbecula – Grimsay – North Uist – Berneray – Harris – Lewis.

As ferries don't run to where the route starts, to get to the start point you'll need to catch a ferry from Oban to Barra and cycle down to Vatersay. From here you can pick up the trail at its southernmost point. Along the route the ferry points all work well, but you'll need to carefully plan your logistics before you go. Much of the riding is also across remote stretches of landscape, so you'll need to make sure you have enough food and water for these. It's worth the planning though – the full crossing is an adventure like no other.

Local Highlights

→ There's so much to see along the route, including Luskentyre Sands, one of the largest and most spectacular beaches on Harris; the Neolithic Callanish (Calanais) Standing Stones on Lewis; Kisimul Castle, standing on an island off Barra; and Traigh Mhor Beach on Lewis, with cottages to stay in right by the sea.

Challenge level: ✪✪✪✪✪
Start: Vatersay, Isle of Barra, HS9 5YL
Finish: Butt of Lewis, HS2 0XF
Distance: 150 miles/241km
Maps: OS Explorer 452, 453, 454, 455, 456, 457, 458, 459 and 460

186

8 Isle of Harris Sea Snorkel Trail ⊕

Harris and Lewis are the largest of the islands in the Outer Hebrides. Sparsely populated, yet rich in cultural heritage, these are fascinating places to visit – wild and rugged, with mountains, windswept moorland and miles of stunning coastline edged with white, sandy beaches and clear, wildlife-rich seas. One of the best ways to explore the coast is by snorkelling, and the Scottish Wildlife Trust has set up several snorkel trails around the north-west Highlands and Harris. There's so much to spot beneath the waves, from small sea squirts, sponges and anemones right up to dolphins, whales and basking sharks.

There are snorkel trails available for all levels, from beginner-friendly sheltered bays to those requiring a longer swim to reach, further out to sea. All are best done in calm conditions for the best visibility and safety. Always check tides, currents and forecasts before you go and never snorkel alone. Use good-quality equipment and wear a wetsuit to keep you warm and protect you from jellyfish stings. Once you're in the water, follow the Snorkeller's Code:

Local Highlights
➡ Stay at the tiny, utterly remote-feeling Cnip Grazing campsite, with fantastic views.
➡ Take part in the Stornoway Half Marathon, which takes place in May.
➡ Sleep in a restored traditional blackhouse (www.gearrannan.com).
➡ Hire a bike and go exploring on two wheels (www.bikehebrides.com).

- Do not remove seaweed or animals from the rock or from their homes.
- Take care not to kick sealife with fins or stand on delicate animals.
- Observe animals where they live and don't take anything away with you.

The North Harris snorkel trail takes in six outstanding snorkelling sites: Hushinish, Seilamol Bay, Aird Asaig, Carragraich Bay, Port Rhenigidale and Loch Mharaig.

Challenge level: ✪✪✪✩✩
Location: various locations in North Harris
Map: OS Explorer 456

188

Hoy is the second-largest island in the Orkney archipelago. Standing close to Rackwick Bay on the west coast of Hoy, the Old Man is a 449-foot (137m) sea stack, one of the tallest of its kind in Britain. It is famous for rock climbing, and the original route, graded E1, was first climbed in a televised ascent by Tom Patey, Rusty Baillie and Chris Bonington in 1966. There are several other harder routes on the stack.

The classic walk to the Old Man of Hoy is an enjoyable and straightforward out-and-back route of nearly 6 miles (10km). Ferries to Hoy will drop you at Moaness, from where you can take a minibus to the beautiful, remote beach at Rackwick Bay – enclosed by red sandstone cliffs, its sands have a pink hue. From here the walk follows the main, signposted track all the way to the Old Man, with outstanding views of the island and surrounding coast throughout. You can either return by the same route or explore further, continuing along the coast to the impressive cliffs at St John's Head, the highest vertical cliffs in the UK. This adds around two hours to the walk. Hoy is also wonderful by mountain bike; from the ferry you can ride across the island to Rackwick Bay – a little over 4 miles (6.4km) – before continuing on to the Old Man.

Local Highlights

→ If you don't fancy leaving Hoy yet, you can stay at Burnmouth Cottage bothy, OS grid ref: ND205987.
→ Refuel at the Beneth'ill Café near the pier at Moaness.

Challenge level: ★★☆☆☆
Start/finish: Rackwick Bay, Hoy
OS grid ref: ND 202992
Distance: 5¾ miles/9.2km
Map: OS Explorer 462

10 Explore Eshaness

In the far north-west of Shetland, the Eshaness peninsula experiences the full force of the North Atlantic, which has sculpted the coastline into an intricate series of stacks, caves, blowholes and geos. The peninsula is the remains of the Eshaness volcano, and you can still see fascinating layers of lava and rock from a volcanic eruption 350 million years ago. Eshaness's breathtaking scenery, diversity of landscape and historical interest, along with its ease of access, make it a great place to explore.

The route: starting at the lighthouse, perched high on an outcrop of volcanic rocks (available as a holiday let), this wonderful loop takes you along the dramatic coast to the head of Calder's Geo, a deep inlet gouged by the sea into the dark rocks. Continue north-east along the coast towards the great, sea-carved hole of Grind of the Navir, with its bouldery beach and strange sea loch. Continue north-east to The Burr, and after Croo Loch head back south-west, reaching the Loch of Houlland and following its western shore. Finish past the twin inlets of Drid Geo and Calder's Geo before returning to the lighthouse.

Local Highlights

➡ Braewick, on Eshaness, has a campsite, café/restaurant and craft shop, with exhilarating views out across the sea stacks (www.eshaness.moonfruit.com).

Challenge level: ✪✪✪✩✩
Start/finish: lighthouse car park, ¾ mile (1.2km) W of B9078 at West Heogaland
OS grid ref: HU 206784
Distance: 4 miles/6.4km
Map: OS Explorer 467

Index

The Adventurer's Guide to Britain

Acknowledgements

Our heartfelt thanks to the amazing outdoor adventure experts who have given their time, knowledge and photographic skills to this project – we couldn't have done it without you. Thanks to Liz Multon for saying yes; Penny Phillips, our brilliant and patient editor; Calvin Evans, who designed the pages; Chris and Clare; Eryl; Lucy, Sam and Osker; Joe and Zana; James and Monika; Paul Wildman Mitchell; Carron Tobin; Mark Bullock; Neil, Adam and Dave; Ordnance Survey and the GetOutside team; Howies and Vaude, whose outstanding ethical kit kept us warm and dry on our adventures; the editing and production team at Bloomsbury; and, as always, to E and H for sharing with us the greatest adventure of all.

Jen and Sim Benson